INTERNATIONAL FOOTBALL BOOK

No. 24

Allan Evans and Tony Morley show off the European Cup they helped Aston Villa win for the first time.

INTERNATIONAL FOOTBALL BOOK

No. 24

Edited by Eric G. Batty

SOUVENIR PRESS LTD. LONDON

First published 1982 by
Souvenir Press Limited,
43 Great Russell Street, London WC1B 3PA
and simultaneously in Canada

ISBN 0 285 62533 0

Photographs by Peter Robinson

Filmset and printed in Great Britain by
BAS Printers Limited, Over Wallop, Hampshire
and bound by Hunter & Foulis Limited, Edinburgh.

Contents

10

Aston Villa win European Cup

English football dominates for six years

With English clubs having held the European Cup for the last five years Aston Villa were not expected to make it six consecutive successes against the West German champions FC Bayern Munich. Villa had earned their place in the final by beating some very good sides and ultimately they rose to the occasion and put their name on the trophy.

Not at any time did the Villa players reproduce the highly entertaining brand of football that had earned them the League championship a year earlier. Dennis Mortimer and Gordon Cowans controlled midfield admirably; Allan Evans produced a really solid performance at the heart of their defence and everyone worked like horses. But the attack, which was Villa's strength, was disappointing. Tony Morley had a subdued match and the central spearheads, Peter Withe and young Gary Shaw, who can be so devastating with their intelligent running, deadly finishing and near perfect understanding, never got going as they can at their best.

Tony Morley (facing page) caught in a ballet scene against Bayern Munich, and, below, Villa manager Tony Barton shows off the coveted European Cup.

Bayern have often been described as a two-man team, relying overmuch on the inspiration of Paul Breitner in an attacking-scoring midfield role, and the smooth as silk skills of Karl-Heinz Rummenigge. But they only flickered from time to time, so the result was almost deadlock.

Villa had their heroes, not least their young giant, 23 years old Nigel Spink who lost his anonymity after only nine minutes. Jimmy Rimmer, solid, reliable and often brilliant over the years, had to quit his goal with an injury collected in training. This turned the spotlight directly on Spink who had previously had only ninety minutes of first team football. But Spink was impeccable. His handling was superb and he collected high crosses under pressure with the calm assurance of a veteran, for surprisingly, the Germans often ended their well constructed attacks with high balls aimed for the heads of their twin strikers, Rummenigge and Dieter Hoeness. That probably gave him the confidence to make several superb saves when Villa were under pressure.

In the second half Villa came under a lot of pressure but the closest Bayern came to scoring was when one effort was headed off the Villa goal-line following a scramble.

The game was won and lost after sixty-seven minutes when Shaw hit a fine pass up the left flank for Morley to beat his man with a flash of skill and pace, to finish with a defence-splitting cross that flashed low across the face of the Bayern goal for Withe to turn it in—off the goalkeeper's left hand post.

Villa were good value for their success though the game never reached any great heights. Manager Tony Barton, almost unknown three months earlier, thus took the club game's most coveted trophy.

Peter Withe, (white shirt), below, scores the only goal in the European cup final, and, facing page, gets another effort on target.

TOTTENHAM retain the F.A. CUP

For the second year in succession the FA Cup Final went to a replay after extra time, and it was Queen's Park Rangers who earned most sympathy from the neutrals after starting as underdogs.

Ranger's goalkeeper Peter Hucker rose to the occasion to play superbly but amongst the outfield players Glenn Roeder was perhaps the best player on the field: marshalling his defence superbly, covering everyone, and also using the ball wisely. Suspended for the re-play, he was badly missed.

The absent Argentinians, Osvaldo Ardiles and Ricardo Villa, were also sorely missed by Tottenham, for this allowed Rangers to concentrate on Glenn Hoddle and by organisation and sheer numerical superiority they cut down the flow of passes going to the Spurs strikers.

And from time to time Rangers broke away themselves in well constructed attacks, even though Ray Clemence in the Tottenham goal was rarely called on. Early in extra time, Glenn Hoddle struck a fine goal, in spite of close attention from Bob Hazell and Tony Currie, and a slight deflection gave Hucker no chance at all.

OPPOSITE Simon Stainrod is dispossessed by Steve Perryman, and below, one of Ranger's heroes, Bob Hazell, sprints to cut off Glen Hoddle.

Mitre
2 5

But six minutes later, when it seemed that the trophy was destined for White Hart Lane, Rangers scored with a neatly worked goal to earn a well deserved equaliser. A throw in by Simon Stainrod was headed on across goal by Hazell and calmly placed into the Tottenham net by Ranger's right back Terry Fenwick.

For the re-play, tickets were on sale at Wembley stadium and for the first time in living memory there was not a capacity crowd. But while the final had been quite easily forgettable, the re-play produced a lot of interesting football, much of it from Rangers; and plenty of incident.

After only six minutes Tottenham went ahead with a penalty from Hoddle. Stainrod lost the ball in midfield to send Graham Roberts on a strong, weaving run towards the goal and, well inside the area, Currie brought him down with a challenge that was clearly illegal. Hoddle's shot, hard and low, put Tottenham in front for the second time and now fate decreed that it was a lead they would not lose.

For much of the first half Spurs were on top but after the break Rangers dominated for half an hour. In this period, Stainrod could have scored with a header when well placed and then Stainrod provided a cross from the left wing from which John Gregory beat Clemence with a first time shot, only to see the ball bounce off the bar. Clemence was kept very busy in this period when Spurs were under intense pressure and Hoddle cleared another effort from Gregory, under his own cross-bar.

Again Gregory clipped the top of the bar with Tottenhm hanging on, but then as so often happens when one team is pressing hard, Tottenham broke away with only one minute left to play and Steve Archibald, through on his own, shot past Hucker, only to see the ball strike a post.

It was not a memorable final from a football viewpoint, but Rangers, though they lost, did their best to make it a good contest, and perhaps deserved better.

Tony Currie (facing page) had a great final for Rangers but conceded the penalty (below) by which Tottenham finally won the F.A. Cup.

During 1981 I watched a lot of international football. Here, based on what I saw, is my world stars team. They are all players of the highest class, so it will be interesting to see how many of them will grace my World XI, chosen after the World Cup was over.

Eric Batty

Goalkeeper ARCONADA (Spain)

ARCONADA of Real Sociedad (San Sebastian) and Spain has been through a three year spell of brilliance that convinced many international critics that he was the best goalkeeper in the World. Like the rest of the Spanish side, he blotted his copy book a little in the recent World Cup, but still left many people unsure whether he or England's Peter Shilton should get the current vote.

Born in San Sebastian on 26th June, 1954, he was christened Luis Maria Arconada Echarri but throughout his football career he has been known simply as Arconada. His father is a wealthy business man, and unusual for a professional footballer, Arconada has studied business methods, accountancy and allied subjects to a high level, so that once his career in goal is over he will be able to take over the family business. In Spain this is not unusual, for even one or two sons of millionaires have played First Division football, though one who starred with Atletico Bilbao refused to accept any payments at all, at his father's insistence, and was rewarded with full caps as an amateur.

Arconada joined Real Sociedad as a boy but as is the Spanish custom was farmed out in his teens to a nearby junior club to gain experience and was recalled in 1974 to make his league debut. When the 1978 World Cup was staged in Argentina he was accorded the number one in Spain's 22 man squad but was kept sitting, frustrated, on the substitute's bench throughout that campaign when manager Ladislav Kubala preferred Real Madrid's Miguel Angel, presumably for his greater experience.

But after that World Cup, Kubala began to turn to him more frequently and when the 1980 European Championship was staged in Italy, Arconada was Spain's undisputed number one. He played superbly in that competition; brilliant when called on to make reflex saves, superb when dealing with high crosses and full of courage when he had to leave his goal and go down at the feet of an oncoming opponent. Arconada 'arrived' on the world stage in that competition and has since played for club and country with great distinction.

He looked superb when Spain visited Wembley in 1981 and won 2–1, taking all the high crosses like a top class English goalkeeper. His confidence spread and undoubtedly he played a key role in his country's success. Having played in the 1976 Olympic Games in Montreal, he was the Spanish captain in the World Cup and for Real Sociedad he has played a major part in their 1981 and 1982 championship successes. Three times he has been awarded the *Trofeo Zamora* as the best goalkeeper in the Spanish League and he has turned down offers of £100,000 a year from Real Madrid and FC Barcelona.

MAGIRUS
DEUTZ

Right back BREITNER (W. Germany)

PAUL BREITNER is probably the best example of the all-round superbly athletic and both skilful and intelligent players that the West Germans seem to produce almost at will nowadays. Born on the 5th September, 1951, he has played for Eintracht Braunschweig and two other lesser known German sides but will be best remembered for his superb performances for FC Bayern Munich and Real Madrid.

Success came to him early for when he was only 19 he helped Bayern win the German FA Cup in 1971, beating 1st FC Köln 2–1 in the final after extra time. Not quite a year later, in April, 1972, Breitner was largely unknown outside Germany when he was one of five Bayern players who helped West Germany beat England 3–1 at Wembley. At the time Breitner was still only twenty years old and that match gave him his fourth cap.

Breitner's chequered career then brought him League championship medals in 1972, 1973 and 1974 and then, finally, success in the European Cup when Bayern beat Atletico Madrid 4–0 in a re-play after a 1–1 draw, again in Brussels.

A former Youth and Under 23 international, Breitner has won every honour open to him in German football and helped beat Holland 2–1 in the World Cup final in 1974 when, at a critical moment with the Germans trailing 0–1, Breitner calmly scored an equaliser with a firmly struck penalty kick.

Although predominantly a right footed player, Breitner played most of his football until then at left back, but was always pressing forward to play a full role and displaying all the skills in his aggressive, attacking style. Then he surprised many people by signing for Real Madrid and helping them to a League and Cup double in 1974–75. He starred, after conversion by the Yugoslav, Miljan Miljanic, as an inside right, playing the midfield general's role, and getting goals freely. The following season he helped Real to retain the championship.

Returning to Bayern in the summer of 1978, Breitner remained in midfield and earned league championship medals in 1980 and 1981, and another FA Cup winner's medal in 1982. In 1981–82 Breitner was Bayern's second highest league goalscorer, but when he returned to the West German side in April, 1981, he played in a defensive midfield role and helped beat Austria by 2–0 in Hamburg.

Breitner is the complete player and all-rounder of proven versatility and now, even close to his 31st birthday he displays almost unlimited stamina. I have chosen him for right back, because he could play there with real distinction and because there is a shortage of really top class full backs.

Clearly one of the outstanding players of the seventies, Breitner earned only 28 caps in that decade because of his four years in Spain. On the ball he displays near perfect control, scores freely with shots, headers and penalty kicks, and off the ball displays a superb positional sense; his anticipation is second to none.

CCCP

Centre back CHIVADZE (Russia)

ALEXANDER CHIVADZE usually presents a dour and taciturn face when approached for an interview by journalists from Western Europe and is probably no different to Russian journalists. But on the field he appears to be light-hearted and gay, frivolous almost, in the eyes of many defensive-thinking Russian officials and coaches.

But this is of course deceptive for in fact he is neither and adopts a very serious approach to the game which is, however, inevitably coloured by his Georgian blood. The Georgians, by temperament, are almost as Latin as the Spaniards or Italians, enjoying their wine and music, and far removed from the typical Russian image in the minds of football fans all over the world.

This image has been created by a series of Russian teams, both clubs and national teams, which destroyed the favourable impression created by the Dynamo Moscow team that toured Britain in 1945 and played flowing, attractive football with the emphasis on attack and scoring goals.

For around thirty years the Russians produced teams that played stereotyped football, based mostly it seemed on physical qualities. The players appeared to be quick, well-trained physically, and defensively well organised, but lacking characters, they played without flair.

Then, after Dynamo Kiev had changed this image more than a little, the European opinion of the Russian footballer was shattered by Dynamo Tbilissi, and their outstanding player was Chivadze. The captain and *libero*, playing the covering role behind the defence, Chivadze surprised everyone by his skill and intelligence. From behind the defence he would burst forward in the manner of Franz Beckenbauer and play a full part in organising attacks in midfield.

Chivadze led Tbilissi to the Russian championship in 1978 for only the second time in their history and four times in the seventies they appeared in the Russian Cup Final, the Cup of the Red Army. Then in season 1980–81 they appeared in the European Cupwinners Cup. Early on they accounted for Kastoria (Cyprus) and Waterford, and then in the quarter finals met West Ham, and shattered all illusions. Coming at the end of their winter break it was expected that Tbilissi would be far below their best, having to play before they had reached peak form by playing league matches.

But away to West Ham, Dynamo Tbilissi were a revelation. Half the team were talented and inventive and at Upton Park, Chivadze steered his colleagues to a totally unexpected 4–1 win. Chivadze gave nothing at all away in defence, far better than Beckenbauer in the air, marshalling his defence like a master and his tackling and covering were superb. But best of all he broke out after intercepting a pass, beat a man in midfield, and stormed upfield on several shattering runs that displayed all his talents—and even scored a superb goal after one of his bursts out of defence with a glorious shot that would have been a worthy 'goal of the season' anywhere.

Born in Tbilissi on 8th April, 1955, Chivadze has only 20-odd caps, but at still only 27 seems destined to get many more.

Centre back STIELIKE (W. Germany)

ULRICH STIELIKE, known to almost everyone as 'Uli', was one of many young players recruited for Borussia Mönchengladbach by Hennes Weisweiler and helped to stardom by him. Weisweiler had a fantastic record with the club, steering them from anonymity into the Bundesliga which began in 1963 without Borussia Mönchengladbach.

Born on 15th November, 1954, Stielike was signed from the unknown junior club SpVgg Ketsch in 1973, after he had earned caps for the West German (amateur) Youth team. He began as a central defender, but Weisweiler converted him into a superb midfield player, cast in the same mould as Beckenbauer and Netzer. But later he switched to play behind the defence and come out into open play like a master-craftsman.

Stielike earned his first full cap for West Germany against Austria in 1975 when he was only twenty. But after helping his club win the Bundesliga title he played against Liverpool in the 1977 European Cup Final and was then, at the end of his contract, transferred to Real Madrid. The fee was a modest one, only £350,000, but Stielike signed a three year contract with the Spanish club, worth a minimum of £120,000 a year.

Before moving to Spain, Stielike had made only six appearances for West Germany and in his first three years in Spain he added only five caps to his tally. But then when his contract came up for renewal he insisted on a clause which guaranteed that he would be released to play in all official international matches and in 1980 he earned five more caps, appearing in all the matches in Italy, both in midfield and as the *libero* and helped win the European Championship.

Since then, under the more liberal regime of Jupp Derwall he has played in almost all the important matches. He looks older than his 27 years, with his slightly balding appearance, but at times the way he plays, he exhibits all the enthusiasm of a youngster. In fact he is endowed with a tremendous will to win, and combines this with a range of subtle skills. The Real Madrid fans have seen the best of Stielike for although he is now a permanent fixture behind their defence, when they are in trouble he is frequently switched to a working-attacking midfield role. A wide range of feints enable Stielike to dribble past almost anyone and he is also deceptively quick.

As a defender he is the complete player, unflappable, decisive, covering all his colleagues in turn, and extremely good in the air. His shrewd distribution marks him as a class player, but in Spain he has picked up the habit of being ruthless, when, as the last man, he fouls opponents who get the ball past him, though never intentionally causing serious injury.

German fans criticised him for going to Spain but who can blame him for wanting to secure his financial future, and in any case all was forgiven long ago; though with Real Madrid he has seldom been in the international spotlight and his best games have been for Spanish eyes only.

It is of course never suggested that he should play at the heart of any defence with Chivadze, but a World XI ought to place the emphasis on class and skill.

Left back JUNIOR (Brazil)

JUNIOR of C.D. Flamengo of Rio de Janeiro and Brazil is surely the best player in his position in the world and an indisputable choice for the I.F.B. team. Born in Joao Pessoa on 29th June, 1954, in the state of Rio, he was christened Junior and not just given the tag as a nickname, as has been reported elsewhere. His full name is Leovegildo Lins Gama Junior, and he is one of swarms of Brazilian stars, both past and present, who played their early football on the Copacabana beach in Rio.

He was, as a youngster, a fan of Flamengo, but he was rather fortunate to end up playing for them. Eager to be a professional, he accepted an offer from another crack Rio club, Botafogo, but after playing in their youth teams they released him in 1973. By then he had made friends with an official of Flamengo, and through this contact he joined the club he had dreamed of playing for as a boy.

Junior began as a midfield player, usually on the left, but often in the centre as an all-rounder where his talents were given full rein. He developed into an accomplished player of superb ability, equally good in defensive duties, as he naturally was at going forward.

In an emergency when the left back was injured in a league game, Junior dropped back and did so well that the manager of the time insisted that he stay in that position. A variety of *tecnicos*, as the Brazilians call the men who prepare and pick their teams, tried at various times to convert him back to midfield but then the arrival of Claudio Coutinho as the Flamengo manager stopped all that. Coutinho could see in him a full back of real class and officially Junior has remained at left back.

But in the recent World Cup in Spain, Junior spent at least as much time in midfield as he did in a defensive role.

After playing in the Montreal Olympic Games soccer series for Brazil, Junior earned a place in Brazil's full side and was well established when, with Brazil, he starred on their 1981 European tour. He showed his class as one of the stars in Brazil's first ever Wembley win over England (1–0) and then scored the winning goal away to West Germany in Stuttgart. Spotting the German substitute goalkeeper, Eike Immel, out of position and off his line at a free kick, Junior chipped the ball over the line of defenders in the wall and in it went off the under-side of the cross bar.

In another victory over West Germany, this time at home, Junior scored a classic goal that proved to be another match-winner. Pushing upfield he received the ball about thirty yards from goal and moving with it he took a one-two off a well placed colleague, raced on and hit home a superb right foot volley.

In 1981 Junior was seen world-wide on television after helping Flamengo win the Rio league championship; the Brazilian title and the South American Club championship, the *Taca de los Libertadores*. That gave Flamengo a place in the world club championship final against Liverpool in Tokio and a world club Cupwinner's medal which was richly deserved.

Right Midfield ARDILES (Argentina)

OSVALDO CESAR ARDILES was born at Cordoba on 3rd August, 1952, and like all the South American stars, developed his superb skills in kick-about games with his friends. Caught in the poverty trap of the Third World we are now seeing players of real ability coming from African and Asian countries, developing along the lines of the Argentinians and Brazilians. For them, football offers them the way out and as well as stardom, a good standard of living that they would surely not have attained without football.

After playing as a professional with Instituo in Cordoba and Huracan of Buenos Aires, he burst onto the world scene with a superb performance for Argentina in the 1978 World Cup. If Mario Kempes took the headlines as the top scorer in Argentina's World Cup winning team, the more discerning critics recognised the tremendous contribution made by Ardiles as the organiser-in-chief, in midfield.

Relieved of all defensive duties, the task of Ardiles in Cesar Menotti's scheme was only to make himself easy to find; to be available for a pass whenever Argentina won the ball. Then, with his superb skills he ran with the ball, beating men and exchanging one-two's with colleagues until he was far enough advanced to lay on the final pass that so often put a striker in for a shot at the enemy goal.

After that World Cup, Tottenham Hotspur very shrewdly beat all opposition and signed Ardiles and his countryman Ricardo Villa, though some people doubted that Ardiles, who is only a little man and slightly built, could survive the hurly-burly in England's highest class. But if anything Ardiles is probably a better all-round player now than he was in 1978 for he adapted his style extremely well. Playing further forward for Tottenham, the spectacular runs with the ball at his feet were no longer a feature of his game. He could not run very far from a more advanced position, but he added a bite and tackling ability to his game, and also scored some very important and skilful goals as well as creating the chances for many more.

Given a free hand in midfield again in the recent World Cup, Ardiles was once more one of Argentina's most important players. His skills, his vision and passing ability stood out, even by comparison with the most gifted Brazilians.

Ardiles was badly missed by Tottenham at the end of last season. Released to prepare for the World Cup after they had reached the FA Cup Final he was prevented from returning by the troubles in the South Atlantic. But there is no doubt that Ardiles was happy with the London club, and in Argentinian football which has been plagued by financial problems there have been many cases of clubs owing salaries and bonuses to their players, and strikes by the players.

There can be no doubting the stature of the little Argentinian in world football and including him in I.F.B.'s World XI along with Zico and Socrates in midfield it is suggested that the team would be unbeatable.

Centre midfield SOCRATES (Brazil)

SOCRATES, of Corinthians (Saõ Paulo) and Brazil, emerged in the recent World Cup as one of the world's most gifted attacking players.

Although predominantly a right footed player he has a wide range of skills and unlike most Brazilian players, when he makes a pass he always moves off to take up another good position and also packs a tremendous wallop when it comes to turning class into goals.

Born at Belem in the state of Parana, close to the Amazon River on 19th February, 1954, he was christened Socrates Brasileiro Sampaio de Sousa Ferreira Oliveira. But when he was five years old his family moved to the major city of Saõ Paulo and he began to join in the games of football played by all the Brazilian youngsters in the streets.

He took to the game as a fish does to water, though he never wore football boots until he was fifteen years old. His first professional club was Botafogo of Ribeiro Preto, not to be confused with the famous Botafogo of Rio de Janeiro, who have provided so many world class players for Brazil, but he was soon transferred when a Corinthians scout spotted his talents.

Twelve months later, Corinthians were the champions of Saõ Paulo and Socrates was awarded his first cap. Corinthians fans and officials were amongst those most critical of Brazil's 1978 manager, the late Claudio Coutinho, for four years ago, Socrates was already a great talent.

But Mr Coutinho had his own ideas about the style that Brazil should play to in Argentina, and there was no place for the young Corinthians star.

Coutinho's critics now claim that his ideas were based on too much theory and that he gave the players lengthy lectures on how the game should be played, insisting that the players follow his orders and play to his ideas.

Socrates is very bright, realising when he was young that he should get a good education, and unusual in these days of specialisation, he is already a fully qualified doctor of medicine.

His Corinthians colleagues were none too happy with the concessions made to Socrates so that he could study, at times, when they were training, but his performances soon won his critics over.

When Tele Santana became the Brazilian manager he included Socrates at once and he scored 12 goals in his first 25 internationals. But though everyone applauded the Brazilians' return to their familiar style with skill predominating above all else, they have not been able to find a suitable centre forward who gets goals regularly at the highest level.

This led to one of Brazil's greatest disappointments—in the *Copa de Oro*—the Gold Cup, staged in Uruguay in December–January of 1980–81. In the final match against Uruguay, who were playing before their own fans, Mr Santana tried Socrates at centre forward, and though they had most of the play and were clearly the better side, they lost 1–2. But with Socrates back in midfield for the World Cup in Spain, it was clear to everyone that Brazil really are still producing great players and Socrates is perhaps the best of the current crop.

10

Left midfield ZICO (Brazil)

ZICO had done so well in the period 1980–81 that he even overhauled the immensely popular Diego Maradona among South American critics, taking the Player of the Year award from him in 1981. This poll is conducted by the newspaper 'El Mundo Deportivo' in Venezuela.

Christened Artur Antunes Coimbra, Zico picked up his nickname as a youngster and retained it on his way to stardom with Flamengo and Brazil. 1981 was his best year yet in terms of titles but overall he has helped Flamengo win the championship of Rio de Janeiro in 1974, 1978, 1979 and 1981 when they went on to earn the Brazilian title and play in the South American club championship which has been largely dominated by Argentinian clubs. Flamengo met Cobreola in the final, losing 0–1 away in Chile but winning 2–1 at home and 2–0 in the play-off, and remarkably, it was Zico who scored all their four goals at that stage.

In 1981 Zico recorded 59 official goals for Flamengo, second highest in the Rio league—three behind Roberto of Vasco da Gama, the centre forward known as 'Dynamita' who had a spell with FC Barcelona. Then of course, Zico was the mastermind behind Flamengo's success over Liverpool in the world club championship final, staged in Tokio. There he was voted the outstanding player in the game and awarded a Japanese car. With Brazil's 'Footballer of the Year' award, he took almost everything in 1981.

Zico is now the most capped player amongst the current Brazilian national players with more than seventy honours and a string of more than fifty goals for Brazil, most of them gems.

He joined Flamengo when he was fifteen years old with four elder brothers all being footballers and three of them reaching First Division standard. But as a teenager, Zico was so slightly built it seemed he might never achieve his ambition and play in the famous Red and Black hoops of Flamengo. Doctors advised a body building course and medication, vitamins and tonics. In 1980, Zico became a target for Spanish and Italian clubs and to keep his services Flamengo had to offer him a reputed £14,500 a month. But his contract expires in 1983 and still only 29 he could well figure in Italy before he retires. To pay his salary, and that of Junior, Flamengo have to play more matches than any other team in the world, for admission prices in Brazil are still very low indeed. As holders of the World Champions title they command big fees for exhibition matches, but now they have practically no time to train and spend as much time flying as they do playing.

Zico first played for Brazil as a striker but in the 1978 World Cup the tactics laid down by manager Coutinho and the European style did not suit Zico's talents; he did however, score against Sweden that unusual headed goal from a corner in 1978 that was disallowed when the referee blew for time between the kick being taken and the ball entering the net. But the more liberal approach of Tele Santana, taking Brazil back to their old, traditional style, enabled Zico to demonstrate all his gifts to the full in the competition in Spain.

Right winger RUMMENIGGE (W. Germany)

KARL-HEINZ RUMMENIGGE of FC Bayern Munich and West Germany is not only one of the most prolific goalscorers in the game today, but certainly the most skilful and elegant. Full-blooded volleys, superb first-time strikes with the outside of his right foot, and even the overhead scissors shot usually associated with South American stars, are amongst his major weapons. Though not particularly good at heading, Rummenigge also gets a good percentage of goals with his head, and unlike many high scorers he very seldom takes penalty kicks to boost his total.

Born on 25th September, 1955, Rummenigge was transferred to Bayern for a mere £4,500 from Borussia Lippstadt in the summer of 1974 as a skilful and very quick right winger. And to underline his development, FC Barcelona offered Bayern what would have been a world record fee of £5 million for him. Rummenigge turned that down, saying quite clearly that money was not everything, although FCB would have paid him an unbelievable figure for a four or five year contract, in salary and bonuses.

Rummenigge won a winner's medal in the European Cup, helping Bayern beat St. Etienne 1–0 in Glasgow in 1976. But he did not find it easy to establish himself in a team dominated by Beckenbauer and Gerd Müller, and Dettmar Cramer had omitted him from the team that beat Leeds United a year earlier in the Paris final. He had to work hard, particularly to improve his heading ability and his left foot skills before he established himself as a super-star.

First capped in the 2–0 win over Wales in 1976, he now has more than fifty international honours, but before Rummenigge established himself he suffered with his colleagues in an unexpectedly difficult time the West Germans experienced in the 1978 World Cup.

Switched to centre forward by Bayern after Müller departed, Rummenigge also figured frequently on the left wing which added to his versatility. Now he roams along the entire attacking front, but is at his best as a right-sided central striker.

Season 1979–80 was Rummenigge's best so far. The top scorer in the Bundesliga with 26 goals, he helped Bayern win the championship. Then he played a vitally important role in the German success in the 1980 European Championship and was voted *Fussballer des Jahres* in Germany and also the European player of the year.

In December, 1981, Rummenigge was again elected the best player in Europe, helped Bayern retain the Bundesliga title in 1980–81 and consistently rejected approaches from all the rich clubs in Italy and Spain.

By 1982 he had developed still further, now becoming a provider of chances for others as well as a striker of superb quality himself. Injuries hampered him in the 1981–82 season but he spearheaded the Bayern attack that won the German FA Cup and scored two superb goals in the European Cup semi-final against CSKA of Bulgaria.

Centre forward SATRUSTEGUI (Spain)

SATRUSTEGUI became first-choice centre forward for Spain after some fine performances for his club Real Sociedad, who play in the northern city of San Sebastian, in the heart of the Basque country. But he has never been accepted by the majority of the fans in Barcelona and Madrid, and there has been more discussion about his inclusion than that of any other player in Spain's 1982 World Cup team.

A year before the *Mundial*, it was clear where the Spanish problems lay, although this did not become really obvious until after the big competition had got under way. But there were some very big hints to those in close contact with the Spanish team, and perhaps manager Jose Emilio Santamaria should have realised it earlier.

In the spring of 1981, Spain earned a well deserved 2–1 victory over England at Wembley, and Satrustegui played a vital part in that success at centre forward.

Although Satrustegui does get goals regularly for his club who have been the Spanish champions for the last two seasons, in 1980–81 and 1981–82, he has not had very much success himself at finding the net for Spain.

Satrustegui's strength was his running off the ball as the Spaniards built up their attacks towards goal. With the ball being shuffled around quickly between the attacking players, Satrustegui created havoc amongst the England defenders by running diagonally across the pitch ahead of them. This pulled the English centre backs out wide, and the Spanish midfield players repeatedly broke through for shots at goal. The Spanish star to the less discerning was midfield man Zamora who hit a fine goal for Spain that evening, though Satrustegui had a big hand in creating the chance.

Zamora and Satrustegui play together for Real Sociedad and have developed an exceptionally good understanding, but he simply does not fit in with the popular Spanish players, right winger Juanito and Barcelona's star striker Quini, who is little more than an orthodox spearhead who puts the ball in the net.

But soon after Spain's Wembley win they met Hungary in Valencia, and there, before an extremely critical crowd they were beaten by 3–0. The difference is that at Wembley, with England pressing forward, Spain could score goals by counter-attacking quickly. The whole Spanish team benefited then from the intelligent running of Satrustegui, as any other well coached team would, but when faced by a defensive-minded Hungary, Spain had to attack, failed to break the visitors down, and were caught themselves by counter-attacks.

That was the start of Spain's problems in the World Cup, and the rest sprang from frustration. But for all his critics, Satrustegui who earned Youth and amateur caps for Spain in his younger days remains a very fine player. Born on 12th January, 1954, Jesus Maria Satrustegui Azpiroz was very harshly treated by the Spanish press.

CCCP

Left winger BLOKHIN (Russia)

OLEG BLOKHIN of Dynamo Kiev and the Soviet Union is undoubtedly the best outside left in the world. Skilful left sided players have always been in short supply, and with wingers largely disappearing from the international scene once more, there is hardly anyone to rival him.

But Blokhin would probably command a place in almost anyone's world team for he has shown over the years that he really is a top class player. His rise to prominence clearly began in the 1974–75 campaign when he played for his club in the European Cupwinners Cup and won the trophy. In the final against Ferencvaros, the Russians won 3–0 and Blokhin and Onitchenko took the Hungarians apart with their swift raiding and intelligent running off the ball. It was an excellent team performance by the Russians, but Blokhin's speed and snap shooting provided the icing on their cake. At the end of 1975, Blokhin was voted European 'Footballer of the Year', a distinction which only the brilliant goalkeeper, Lev Yachin, had previously taken to the Soviet Union.

Blokhin has earned every honour open to him in the Russian game, taking a string of winner's medals in their championship and FA Cup; earning the best player award and been the top league goalscorer several times in each.

Born in Kiev on 5th November, 1952, Blokhin was not the first Ukrainian to star in Dynamo Kiev's drive to domination of the Russian game, but he was the first from that club to get goals regularly. With tremendous left foot shots; curling free kicks, and quite a few headed goals, Blokhin finally became Russia's highest ever goalscorer in the history of their game. In the 1981 season he helped Dynamo beat Spartak Moscow 2–0 and the second goal came from him. That gave him a grand total of 153 goals in league matches and beat the all-time record of Alexander Ponomaryov who reached 152 for Torpedo Moscow before retiring after the 1956 campaign.

Blokhin's achievement is all the more remarkable because he scored most of his goals when Russian league football was almost as negative and dominated by defensive tactics as the Italian game. He has of course been very tightly marked and often brutally treated by defenders.

With modern tactics unlikely to change, and Blokhin being only 28 when he became Russia's highest ever league scorer it seems a near certainty that his tally will never be beaten, for he isn't finished yet. He is also the all-time most successful marksman for Russia in international matches. With more than thirty international goals from around eighty games, he has left behind the total of Valentin Ivanov (Torpedo Moscow) who had scored 26 times for Russia.

Blokhin's early years saw him more involved with athletics than football, a sprinter with promise. His mother had been an 80 metres hurdles champion and he is now a fully qualified teacher of Physical Education. He recently married a young Kiev gymnast who had been a world champion in her sphere and an enormous crowd of Dynamo fans turned out for the civil ceremony. And since he began playing for Dynamo, the Kiev club has been the best supported team in Russia.

Substitute SCHUSTER (W. Germany)

BERND SCHUSTER of FC Barcelona and West Germany burst into prominence during the 1980 European Championship, and was clearly a great find. That a player with his gifts can be produced in Western Europe disproves the theory that only the South Americans can now develop really talented stars. It has been argued, with some justification, that youngsters in Europe, with so many other things to spend their time on, do not develop the skills their forefathers had because they do not put in the hours of kicking a ball around when young. But the emergence of Schuster as a super-star proves this is not so.

In 1980, West German critics immediately began to compare him with Franz Beckenbauer, for Schuster is able to play equally well as an attacking midfield player; getting well forward to score frequently, and also an excellent *ausputzer* as the Germans call their free back, playing behind the defence.

Schuster was born in Ludwigshafen on 22nd December, 1959, but when he was very small his family moved to Augsburg. When he was six years old he joined a junior club in the town and soon attracted the attention of FC Augsburg who were at the time playing in the West German Bundesliga. While with them he earned Youth caps and aroused the interest of most of the big, well known German clubs. Eventually, in 1978, he agreed to be transferred to 1st FC Köln who were at the time, the reigning champions.

Hennes Weisweiler, then the trainer of the Cologne club, gave young Schuster a place in the first team almost immediately and in that 1978–79 season he made his debut for West Germany in a 3–1 win against the Republic of Ireland, in Dublin.

Jupp Derwall had been the manager of the German Youth team when Schuster was capped at that level, and it was Derwall, having taken over from Helmut Schön in 1978, who gave him his first full caps. But though he had been around a little while, his performance in the 1980 European Championship took most foreign observers by surprise. Early in 1980, Schuster scored a magnificent goal against Poland after going on as substitute but he did not get a place in the team for the opening match in Italy. Then, against Holland, Herr Derwall brought him in and he had a hand in all three goals. But he also received a yellow card, and that was probably the reason why he was omitted from the unimportant match against Greece (0–0) but brought back to star in the final in which the Germans beat Belgium by two goals to one.

Since then, Schuster hit both goals when the Germans won 2–0 away to Albania but then, with FC Barcelona, declined further caps after a dispute it is said with Breitner. But in Spain Schuster played superbly and when it seemed that Barcelona must win the league his injury struck and while his future was placed in doubt, FCB's challenge faded and came to nil.

Italy win the World Cup

The 1982 World Cup has come and gone, and generally it was very disappointing. For one thing, no new great stars emerged, and many of the established players performed far below their best. Many of the games – too many – were quite boring in fact.

This was especially true, for example, of the first round clash between Italy and Poland which was drawn 0–0, in Vigo. Watching Spain, who as the home country began as one of the favourites, must have given neutrals a pain. And millions around the world, watching on television, must frequently have been tempted to switch off. Only the faint hope that something good might happen any minute, probably kept the vast majority from doing so.

The final itself should be, and is expected to be, a classic encounter, showing off all the best things in world football, demonstrated by super-stars. But, particularly in the first half it was just one long yawn.

The majority of the people I know agreed that the best possible final, from a football viewpoint, and the provision of an entertaining and exciting game, would have been between Brazil and France. They were the two most popular teams with neutrals.

When watching Brazil, one always had a feeling of expectancy, wondering which player was going to surprise us next with a surge upfield, a feint, or a mazy dribble.

Before getting on to the football, let me give FIFA and their Organizing Committees, two great big black marks.

First, the manner in which the match tickets were distributed was a disgrace, resulting in unsold and empty seats, in one instance even for a Brazil match!

Then of course there was the refereeing, which was nothing less than diabolical. I believe that FIFA were fortunate that two basic decisions did not have serious consequences.

The first was to be democratic, and give the 'middle' to referees from some of the African and Asian countries, as well as Central Americans, in the first round matches.

Then there was the old problem of having men accustomed to being in the middle with the whistle, holding the flags on the touchlines.

The requirements of the two tasks are quite different. The referee has to take a general view of the play, and very largely follow the ball. Linesmen on the other hand, should in theory concentrate on the ball being in or out of play; watch off-the-ball incidents going on behind the referee's back, and above all, signal for off-sides.

Throughout the tournament there were many very dubious off-side decisions, and I believe that these stemmed from having referees doing the lines. The officials cannot change their habits, like switching on and off a light,

OPPOSITE Dino Zoff, the goalkeeper and captain of Italy, holds aloft the world's premier trophy.

and the linesmen generally were watching the play.

Then, suddenly, they would look up and see a player receiving the ball in an off-side position, and up would go their flags. But the essence of the off-side law is where that player was at the moment the ball was played, and I am quite sure that in fact, many players who were given off-side, were on-side when the ball was played.

This is not a new problem, nor will it be easily solved. It has plagued World Cups, on and off, for at least thirty years to my certain knowledge.

The only real answer is to ask each country to nominate two or three men who are currently acting as linesmen, and appoint them to take the flags.

As far as the referees are concerned I agree it is more difficult than ever to please everyone and be one hundred per cent right all the time. Too many players today 'dive' in the penalty areas.

Again there was the question of pretending to be seriously hurt, in an attempt to waste time. FIFA has always been consistent about this, to my knowledge. In all the World Cups I have seen, going back to 1954 in Switzerland, the referees have been instructed to follow the laws of the game. These state quite clearly that unless the referee has reason to believe that a player is very seriously injured, he should not allow anyone to give him treatment of any kind on the pitch. The player should go to the touch line, or be carried there, in order not to waste time.

It would help a lot if referees were instructed to wave a stretcher on when the ball went out of play. And then, if any player declined to be carried off, he should be shown the yellow card!

If you observe a number of games carefully, you will surely notice that it is the players from the teams that are winning who try to waste time in this way. Players of losing teams always do their best to struggle on if they possibly can.

Generally the referees were very inconsistent. Some of them flashed yellow cards if players did not retreat the statutory ten yards at free kicks, while others did not. And then of course, all the players in the wall, having got back ten yards, immediately begin to shuffle their feet and edge forward. Watch them in league games.

The answer would be to adapt the Law and give referees the power to move the free kick five yards closer to the defender's goal . . . if they did not all retreat the obligatory ten yards—at once.

Finally, before leaving this theme, Spain were, as the home side usually is, very kindly treated by referees. They looked to be in very serious trouble, losing one-nil to little Honduras in their opening match, when the referee gave them a doubtful penalty.

Then, in their second match against Yugoslavia, they not only got another penalty decision that looked wrong, but also had the benefit of taking it again because the goalkeeper moved when the spot kick was placed wide. Juanito scored at the second attempt and this was the only game that Spain won.

When it came to the penalty shoot-out after extra time between France and West Germany, it was obvious that both goalkeepers were moving before the

OPPOSITE, Klaus Fischer the German centre forward gets an effort on target in the final but Zoff gets down to his left hand to turn the ball away.

BRAND
canon

penalties were taken, but not one was ordered to be re-taken, and neither goalkeeper was cautioned.

Now, having got all that off my chest, back to the football, grim though much of it was.

The really outstanding players were very few and in my opinion there was not one really good team in Spain.

For the best players I would have difficulty choosing between two Brazilians, the elegant and skilful Socrates and the exceptionally gifted and intelligent Falcaõ. Excellent in a slightly different way was their colleague Toninho Cerezo. He was very good on the ball, but also made excellent penetrative runs when he did not have possession of the ball. One that I will not easily forget came in the match against Italy when Brazil equalised to make the score 2–2. Falcaõ had the ball, approaching the Italian penalty area, but his path towards goal was blocked by a mass of blue shirts. Then, almost from nowhere, Toninho Cerezo sprinted round the outside of the Italian defence, on Brazil's right wing. At once, three Italian defenders moved to their left, expecting that he would receive a pass, and that opened the road to goal for Falcaõ, who shifted the ball onto his left foot before driving in a fine goal.

Another memorable goal was scored by Brazil, this time by Junior, who had a comparatively disappointing World Cup. Against Argentina, Junior won the ball near the half-way line and pushed the ball to a colleague on his right, and immediately sprinted away towards goal. The ball was shifted further right by Brazil before a glorious through ball was laid that completely split the Argentinian defence . . . and there was Junior to pick up the ball and calmly roll it home past Fillol.

The South Americans were generally very disappointing. For Argentina only Daniel Passarella and Osvaldo Ardiles were outstanding, while the much-boosted Diego Maradona had a terrible time. Being sent off in Argentina's final match in Spain simply tied a nice black ribbon around Maradona's 1982 adventure.

But in his defence I must say that he is at his best as an attacking player in midfield. With Mario Kempes clearly finished as a goal-getter and no one else able to fill this role, Maradona's boss, Cesar Luis Menotti, pushed him up to centre forward, and this is simply not his game. He will, at his best, get goals going forward, but he does not have either the temperament or the know-how to play at centre forward.

For Peru, who looked so good before the World Cup, it ended in a shambles. In my opinion, the performances of their best forwards, Cesar Cueto and Cesar Luis Uribe, were badly affected by tight-marking opponents and some dirty play. Uribe in particular, who scores most of their goals, got a terrible kicking in their opening match against Italy. That probably left him half fit but certainly lacking in confidence for the rest of the tournament.

Cueto, in midfield still produced some deft touches, but Uribe had little room to move around and shake off his marker. He had to stay upfield and take it and he clearly did not like it.

OPPOSITE Leandro, the Brazilian right back beats Italy's Francesco Graziani to set up another Brazilian attack.

Peru's Argentina-born goalkeeper, Ramon Quiroga, let them down on several occasions too. He can be brilliant at saving shots, but several times he raced out of his goal to invite an oncoming opponent to score easily. This was never more apparent than in the decisive first round match against Poland when he sprinted out to give Grzegorz Lato an empty goal to aim at.

And so to Brazil, who with West Germany were my tips to reach the final. I had been very impressed by the Brazilians in 1981, who in the spring of that year showed they could travel to Europe without losing anything. In a rapid tour they beat England, France and West Germany, even without Falcaõ who was not released by his Italian club AS Roma.

But then they had Reinaldo at centre forward, and if he was not a superior class player, he was not a bad one. Then he got a serious injury and manager Tele Santana tried half a dozen centre forwards in the second half of 1981.

The one he finally chose, the big, black, and predominately left footed Serginho, just did not fill the bill. He was very raw and his distribution left very much to be desired. I still cannot make up my mind whether he or goalkeeper Valdir Peres was Brazil's worst player.

The Brazilians were super-fit, one of the benefits of their lengthy preparations, and they did not seem to mind the oppressive heat that clearly bothered many other teams.

I thought the Russians had them in serious trouble in their very first match in Spain. A goal down at the interval, Brazil were very fortunate not to be out of it then, for in my opinion, the Russian, Shengelia, was clearly held inside the penalty area, for a penalty that was not awarded by an awful Spanish referee.

Brazil made a magnificent come-back against the visibly tiring Russians and superbly struck long shots by Socrates and Eder gave them a belated 2–1 win.

Against Scotland, who at the time seemed to play it just right at the start, the Brazilians were again in difficulties. David Narey gave the Scots a 1–0 lead to justify manager Jock Stein's choice, and once more it took a long time for the Brazilians to settle down. One each at half time, the Brazilians were clearly superior in terms of craft and skill, but in retrospect I wonder, could Scotland have beaten them if they had attacked what turned out to be a very, very suspect Brazilian defence?

The Scottish players were just as badly affected by the heat of Seville as the Russians had been, and in the end Brazil won at a canter by 4–1.

Already sure to be winners of their group before their final first round match against New Zealand, Socrates & Co. showed little urgency in their play but finally strolled to a comfortable 4–0 victory.

The second phase turned out to be very poorly balanced. There were two evenly balanced groups—Poland, Russia and Belgium in Group A in Barcelona, and Group B in Madrid that brought West Germany, England and Spain together. Then in Group D there was a very easy group at Madrid with France, Austria and Northern Ireland being thrown together and an extremely difficult group in Barcelona: Brazil, Italy and Argentina.

OPPOSITE Italy's left back, Antonio Cabrini moves upfield to start a counter-attack.

To make matters worse, the Group A games were staged before meagre

crowds at FC Barcelona's Nou Camp while the matches between Brazil, Argentina and Italy were staged at RCD Espanol's tiny little Saaria stadium which holds less than half the spectators that can be accommodated at the Nou Camp.

Argentina were the first to fall foul of the Italians and lost 2–1 after a goal-less first half. But it was a very dirty game, and the referee proved that he had no control by allowing Argentina's goal, struck from a free kick by Passarella. When the Argentinian struck his shot the referee was still trying to organise the wall of Italian defenders and had not given the signal to take the kick. Strictly he should have ordered the free kick to be taken again, but I did not object because I really hate the way the Italians play . . . cynical, dirty, time-wasting when they are ahead.

After Brazil had beaten Argentina 3–1 the final Group C match between Italy and Brazil was one that the Italians had to win. A drawn match would have seen Brazil go into the semi-finals on goals difference.

So just for once the Italians were forced to attack. Badly informed, alleged experts, have praised the Italians for the manner in which they disposed of Brazil, singing their praises and talking, and writing, a lot of drivel about the Italian's new-style, attacking football.

Believe me, if it had been the other way around with Brazil needing to win in order to qualify we would have seen Italy play as they usually do, defending in strength with nine men in their penalty area, and perhaps pushing forward two or at the most four players from time to time.

We saw the true, typical Italian performances in their first round matches when they drew 0–0 with Poland, 1–1 with Peru and 1–1 with Cameroon. And anyone who believes that the Italians, whether club or country, are now going to play more openly and attractively is really kidding himself.

Unfortunately for real football, the Brazilians were found wanting, both in attack and at the back. Paolo Rossi gave Italy the lead. Twice the Brazilians trailed, and twice they equalised through Socrates and Falcaõ, but Rossi proved what a fine centre forward he is by completing a hat-trick, after failing to score in Italy's three opening matches.

Clearly Rossi is a fine player, but we knew that years ago. It was quite remarkable that after just a few games he should recapture his outstanding finishing skills following a two year lay off.

The Brazilian attack just did not exist and with their defence cut apart almost every time that Italy pushed forward, everything hinged on their four midfield stars: Socrates, Falcaõ, Zico and Toninho Cerezo.

Zico clearly did not like being tightly marked, and little was seen of him in this match. The other three were quite brilliant, but manager Santana must have realised that his strength was in going forward from midfield.

It would have been against the Brazilians' nature to play defensively, and I personally doubt their ability to defend.

That would have been disastrous but even so the Brazilians showed their innocence when with the score at 2–2 they did not try to play 'Keep the ball'. If

OPPOSITE Zbigniew Boniek (Poland) steps past the beaten Ludo Coeck (Belgium) in the 1982 World Cup game in which Boniek scored a hat trick to beat Belgium 3–0.

OPPOSITE Action from the 1982 World Cup opening game in which Belgium beat Argentina 1–0. On the ground is Vereauteren of Belgium who can only watch as Argentina's Olguin slips away with the ball.

they had done that in their own half and around the half way line, they might just have hung on to draw and go on to win the World Cup as all neutrals wanted them to.

But the Brazilians are not even adept enough, or nasty enough to do that. They went, almost like lambs to the slaughter, and they forced Italy to produce several attacking moves of quality that few other countries could have done. Brazil went out, but they went down gloriously, playing and trying to play, real, old-fashioned open football.

The only other team to play really open football (just once) was little El Salvador who were hammered 10–1 by the Hungarians in their first match. This incidentally is an all-time record score for any World Cup, but digesting the lessons of that first encounter in Europe, El Salvador then made it much harder for Belgium, runners-up in the 1980 European Championship who could only win by 1–0.

Then when it came to Argentina, El Salvador again tried to lock the doors to their goal but were beaten 2–0. Pulling men back to pack their penalty area, El Salvador really tried to keep Belgium and Argentina out by purely defensive tactics and a lot of hard work.

* * *

Maradona might well have thought he would have an easy romp and perhaps establish a new personal goal-scoring record for one World Cup game, but in fact he even failed to score and on top of that the Argentinians' opening goal came from a very doubtful penalty, converted by Passarella. Then Daniel Bertoni scored a fine individual goal to complete the scoring. El Salvador had learned the hard way.

Kuwait, Algeria and Cameroon all created a good impression, underlining my long-held conviction that the Africans will rule the football world if they get themselves better organised, coach properly and ensure the physical condition of their youngsters. Algeria beat West Germany 2–1 and then failed to qualify on goals after the quite scandalous Germany-Austria 'no contest' match. Cameroon got three points just like Italy, but had a 1–1 tally to Italy's 2–2—so out they went. They will come again.

One of the big surprises on the positive side was the success of Northern Ireland, the country with the smallest population of all the twenty-four finalists.

Against all the odds, Billy Bingham's men not only reached the second round but actually topped their group.

To do that they began with a 0–0 draw against Yugoslavia who were extremely disappointing. The skilful Yugoslavs did everything up to the penalty area but after that they wanted to walk the ball into the net. Especially disappointing was Zlatko Vujovic from Hajduk Split who had been their sole regular scorer in the qualifying competition, and he had an awful World Cup.

Slowing the game down in the unaccustomed heat, the Irish played very sensibly and economically. They built up their attacks with short ground passes, being especially careful not to give the ball away in their own half which

would have forced all their players to spring back and expend their invaluable energy. Having worked the ball forward, with Sammy McIlroy playing a vitally important rôle and David McCreery working like a beaver, they proved to be very hard to beat. In attack they often used the high cross to good advantage, for none of their three first round opponents looked comfortable under pressure in the air.

Pat Jennings in the Irish goal, and Jim Platt when Jennings was injured, came to their rescue with several good saves at critical moments, and also the running and skill of Gerry Armstrong, who scored two vital goals against Honduras and Spain, underline that their success was not entirely due to the luck of the Irish.

They were fortunate, as it turned out, to be drawn against an ineffective Yugoslavia and an inexperienced Honduras—compared for example with Scotland. But they covered themselves with glory, when in their final qualifying round match, they beat Spain 1–0 at Valencia to top their group with a two-one goals tally from their three matches.

In the second round Northern Ireland put up a brave battle against Austria in their opening match. After leading 1–0 at the interval with a goal from Billy Hamilton, they found themselves 1–2 down, but with a tremendous will to win they forced their tired bodies to run in the heat of Madrid and fought back to draw 2–2.

Then of course they came up against a confident and skilful French team that put them firmly in their place by four goals to one. But the Irish players can take pride in the fact that they achieved what England failed to do—in beating Spain—and they ensured that the Irish FA has no financial problems for some years to come. Their share of the FIFA takings will be an enormous boost to their normal income.

Scotland had a formidable task before they even arrived in Spain, drawn in the Southern Group 6 with Brazil, Russia and New Zealand. After beating New Zealand by five goals to two, their fans were very concerned about the two goals they conceded. One was a glorious error, first by captain and right back Danny McGrain whose pass back to goalkeeper Alan Rough was nothing like strong enough, and the goalkeeper did nothing to help save the situation.

In the event, those two goals proved to be of vital importance, for when it was all over Scotland went out with an inferior goals difference to the Russians who took second place. Had Scotland beaten New Zealand by 5–0, then, unless the Russians had been stirred into scoring more goals against New Zealand, the Scots would probably have gone forward into the second round through having scored more goals than Russia.

Scottish manager Jock Stein brought down a car-load of criticism on himself by omitting Kenny Dalglish, but in my opinion he was probably right. Though Dalglish has been Liverpool's best player since he left Celtic, he has very rarely played at his best when wearing the Scottish shirt.

His replacement against the Russians was big Joe Jordan and when presented with a gift chance he took it really well to put the Scots one up and give all his colleagues a psychological lift when they needed it most. In the end however, with both sides clearly affected by the stifling heat, they could only draw 2–2

OPPOSITE England beat France 3–1 in Bilbao and Terry Butcher (4) sweeps scorer Bryan Robson up into the air while Frenchman Battiston looks on in disgust.

OPPOSITE Action from the game in which Northern Ireland's World Cup campaign ended. Mal Donaghy (light shirt) and Gerard Soler of France, tussle for the ball.

with Russia and went out on goals difference.

I was not one of those gloomy people who predicted that England would have a tough time qualifying from their group against France, Czechoslovakia and Kuwait. In fact, soon after the draw was made I wrote in the English monthly magazine 'World Soccer' that the England players would deserve a good kicking if they did not reach the second round.

However, when I wrote that, I did qualify it by saying that in my opinion the most important English players were Kevin Keegan and Trevor Brooking and I do not take either statement back.

England received a very early boost when Bryan Robson struck a superb volley against France and after Soler had made it 1–1 he struck again with a fine header. Then a gift goal by Paul Mariner, presented to him by Marius Tresor, wrapped up a hard earned 3–1 win.

Then, against Czechoslovakia it was clear to me that the Czechs were very nervous. They have never been happy playing away from home against British teams, and as things turned out, although they kept the score-sheet blank until half time, they then gave away two gift goals. First the Czech goalkeeper allowed a high ball to go right through his hands; a ball that he should certainly have held, and it fell just right to present Trevor Francis with an open goal that he volleyed home. Then all doubts disappeared when the Czech full back Jozef Barmos turned a mis-hit shot by Mariner into his own net, with the goalkeeper naturally going the wrong way to meet the shot and unable to recover.

Then England made hard work of their final match against Kuwait, even though they knew before the start that whatever the outcome they would not only qualify for the second stage but also go forward as group winners.

But as we have so often seen, England struggled in attack against a side that varied its defensive tactics between an Italian-style *libero*, and an off-side trap. This combination is guaranteed to confuse even the best English players—and it did.

With England thus qualified for the second stage they were unfortunate to find themselves in a group with West Germany and Spain who were of course on home ground.

The Germans played very carefully, anxious not to give anything away, and their well organised defence gave the English attack the usual problems. Only very late in the game did the Germans show any real desire to move forward, and a rare lapse in the England rearguard could have cost them dear.

They allowed Karl-Heinz Rummenigge to turn on a ball and get a good look at the England goal, and he produced a longe range shot which cannoned off the England cross-bar with Peter Shilton well beaten for the only time in the competition.

Then came the match that England had to win by two clear goals against Spain, after the West Germans had beaten them 2–1.

By that time the Spanish players knew that no matter what, their interest in the competition was now over, and all their nerves disappeared. Anxious to please their supporters by putting England out—partly because the Spanish

20
3

crowd was anti-British over Gibraltar and the Falklands—the crowd got behind the Spanish players.

Late in the game, too late in my opinion, Keegan and Brooking were sent on and for the first time they began to cause the Spanish defenders some discomfort. But the goals did not come, and England were as bad in the second round as they had been good in the first.

Shilton vied with Renat Dasajev, the Russian goalkeeper, as the best in the competition, but the only other England players to please me were Ray Wilkins . . . and Robson in the first round.

Having handed out the plaudits I must also confess that I thought that Rix and Francis were both terrible, and Mariner was not up to England standard either.

The West Germans were also very disappointing, but remembering how little was contributed to the European Cup Final by Paul Breitner and Karl-Heinz Rummenigge, and knowing that they both missed league matches near the end of the season, I now feel that they have been carrying injuries and been only half fit for some time. And just for the record I am not at all impressed by either of the Forster brothers or by that big bundle of muscles, Hans Peter Briegel.

And so to the final which I must confess was terribly boring in the first half, and in which it was clear that Rummenigge was unfit. He proved that by going off, and the Germans were also no doubt affected by having to play thirty minutes extra time against France in the semi-final.

But on the day ultra-defensive Italy were the better of two very poor sides and if they deserved to win, their success does not please me. Now more than ever, other countries, and many clubs, will try to play the Italian way, and that cannot be good for football.

Of course Bruno Conti is a very good player, quick, skilful and bright. And Paolo Rossi at his best is a centre forward who relies not on height and physical qualities but on his skills, intelligence and anticipation.

The Italians have always had some very gifted players, especially defenders, but the tactics they adopt are often questionable. And if manager Enzo Bearzot is so keen on good football, why does he not kick out hard-men like Fulvio Collovati and Claudio Gentile?

This is not to say that on the evidence of the final alone the Italians did not deserve to win, but no one will ever convince me that for all their skills they are the best football team in the world.

Leading goal scorers in the 1982 World Cup:

Rossi (Italy)	6
Rummenigge (West Germany)	5
Boniek (Poland)	4
Zico (Brazil)	4
Armstrong (N. Ireland)	3
Kiss (Hungary)	3
Falcaõ (Brazil)	3
Giresse (France)	3

Having chosen a World XI for 1981 and provided biographies earlier in this book, I give below my WORLD CUP XI, which underlines, as Paolo Rossi did, that even a week can be a long time:

SHILTON (England)
DUARTE (Peru)
TRESOR (France)
PASSARELLA (Argentina)
GIRESSE (France)
ARDILES (Argentina)
FALCAÕ (Brazil)
SOCRATES (Brazil)
PLATINI (France)
RUMMENIGGE (West Germany)
ROSSI (Italy)

Leading Goal-getters in all the World Cups to date

1930	Stabile (Argentina)	8
1934	Schiavio (Italy)	4
	Nejedly (Czechoslovakia)	4
	Conen (Germany)	4
1938	Leonidas (Brazil)	8
1950	Ademir (Brazil)	7
1954	Kocsis (Hungary)	11
1958	Fontaine (France)	13
1962	Garrincha (Brazil)	4
	Ivanov (Russia)	4
	Vava (Brazil)	4
	Jerkovic (Yugoslavia)	4
	Sanchez (Chile)	4
	Albert (Hungary)	4
1966	Eusebio (Portugal)	9
1970	Müller (West Germany)	10
1974	Lato (Poland)	7
1978	Kempes (Argentina)	6
1982	Rossi (Italy)	6

European League and Cup Survey

All the post-war details, across Europe, with all the leading league scorers

Last season's experiment in English football, awarding three points for a win in a league match, was adjudged a success after initial scepticism. In the final weeks of the campaign, when interest is usually flagging, the crowds were persuaded to keep coming because almost until the last day, practically every club in the First Division was involved, either in the hunt for a place in the UEFA Cup, or in the battle against relegation.

But the English were not the first to give three points for a league win. This distinction belongs to Greece, though they introduced the scheme for very different reasons. Their game was marred, almost week after week, by rioting crowds who disagreed with the decisions of referees, or by players who were sent off but refused to leave the field.

So they decided to give three points for a win, but added two extra twists. In a match that was drawn, each team received two points, and the losers were awarded one point as a consolation, as long as the match went the full ninety minutes. If a match had to be abandoned for any reason, then no points were awarded. The idea was partially successful, usually in preventing teams walking off the pitch when, near the end of a match, a referee awarded a penalty or other disputed goal which meant defeat. By staying on the pitch the losing team received one point.

Why this step was necessary is underlined by the example of an FA Cup semi-final in 1964. The match was a local derby between Panathinaikos, the most popular club in Athens, and Olympiakos, who play in the adjacent town of Piraeus, which is the port of the capital.

With the score standing at 1–1 the fans were annoyed by a referee's decision and swarmed onto the pitch. Bottles and boxes, taken from beer stalls, were hurled onto the pitch; safety fences were torn down and the pitch invaded, and with the goals uprooted and litter everywhere the ground looked like a battlefield.

The previous season when these same two clubs met in a league match there was an even worse riot with three dead; more than one hundred detained in hospital and another one hundred arrested. The players and referee locked themselves in the stand until police reinforcements arrived and dispersed the crowd with tear gas.

But the Greek temperament is such that even the loser's point was not enough on one occasion, even in the most unusual circumstances. On the last day of the season, Panathinaikos were three points clear at the top and could not possibly be overtaken. With one point from their last match they were certain to stay on top of the table, even if their challengers won their last game. All they had to do

OPPOSITE Pol Van Himst, Belgium's top league scorer for the first-time in 1963–64 and so often the hero, as scorer or schemer, for Belgium and RSC Anderlecht.

was complete their last match in an orderly fashion—if they could not win—and the championship would be assured by the loser's consolation point.

They were in fact losing the final match, away from home, but that did not matter until, near the end, one of the Panathinaikos players was sent off . . . and refused to leave the field!

The referee threatened to abandon the game and though his team-mates, the manager, and even the club chairman, all pleaded with the player to come off, he refused. Panathinaikos were still champions on that occasion for their rivals for the title failed to win, but it does underline the problems faced by the Greek Football Association.

There has been one other variation from the usual two points for a win formula, which is reflected in the Russia championship records. By the early 1970's the game in the Soviet Union was almost as defence-orientated as the Italian game. In an attempt to encourage more open, attacking football, the Russian authorities introduced an unusual innovation. After ten drawn league matches, any club drawing further matches did not receive the customary point for a draw. It made little impact however, and the clubs continued to play to avoid defeat, and win if they could. But with defensive tactics still paramount perhaps the Russians will now try something else.

In common with many other countries, the Russians do not like goal average when two teams finish level at the top on points. They stage a play-off game between the two teams finishing level at the top on points, and for example in 1970, CSKA are shown as champions. The team of the Headquarters of the Russian Army—Central House of the National Army—CSKA Moscow finished level at the top with Dynamo Moscow. The play-off was drawn 0–0, but they then won a second play-off by 4–3 to take the championship trophy.

Many other countries take a similar view of goal average, referred to as 'those damned dots', though several countries do accept goals difference; awarding the higher place to the team that scores most goals.

Unfortunately these things cannot be shown in the tables for each country, but some of the variations can be explained here.

One of the countries with their own regulations for settling the positions of clubs who finish level at the top is Belgium. There they refuse to consider goals at all and award the title to whichever of the two level clubs has chalked up the most victories in league games.

The Dutch took a similar view to the Russians in 1958 when DOS Utrecht ended up level on points at the top with SC Enschede. A play-off was arranged and DOS Utrecht took the title with a 1–0 win.

Then, in Poland, only last season, Widzew Lodz, the reigning champions, took the league title again, because of their own answer to the problem. There the ruling is that when two teams finish level on points, anywhere in the league table, the higher place is awarded to the team that did best in the two league encounters between the two teams level on points.

With regard to the goal scorers who top the list in each country, there are some gaps for which I must apologise. This is absolutely unavoidable in those

OPPOSITE The brilliant Hungarian forward Ferenc Bene, who was his country's top league scorer for the first time in season 1962–63. After more than twenty years with Ujpest Dozsa, Bene played in Finland last season – 1981

countries where no records have been kept. For example, in Wales their national league is competed for by non-league clubs and by the reserve teams of clubs like Swansea City and Newport County, and I have been unable to find anyone who has the list of the top goalscorers.

In Malta there are some gaps in this section. The list was compiled for me by the Maltese journalist Charles Camenzuli, but even he has not been able to provide a complete list going back to season 1945–46. No one at the Malta FA can help either, and I understand that when FA officials have queries from the past, they refer to Mr. Camenzuli!

This is the case too for the first two seasons after the war in Belgium. No records were kept, no newspaper or annual has ever published the figures and neither the press nor the FA can fill these two gaps.

In Holland it was a similar story. Travelling in Holland, watching matches in the fifties, and also attending training sessions and talking to all kinds of people, I was repeatedly told, 'Of course football is only a game. Work comes first.'

At that time the Dutch were all amateurs, but I remember too seeing a game at Geleen in 1955. There the local club was known as Fortuna '54 who, with Ajax and Feyenoord were amongst the leaders in a revolution against the Royal Dutch Football Association.

The FA refused to allow professionalism, so a group of clubs got together and forming their own professional league, broke away from the FA and played for a while as Pirates.

Eventually, peace was made, and the clubs agreed to limit the number of professionals at first. But unofficially they paid more than the permitted number and slowly it died a natural death and professionalism was accepted.

This led of course to the Super-Ajax who followed Feyenoord by winning the European Cup and produced some of the finest football seen anywhere in the world. And of course the Dutch side in the 1974 World Cup which was so widely acclaimed, could never have achieved what they did as amateurs.

But now there are clear indications that the fears of the FA officials who stood out against professionalism are justified. The majority of the clubs in the Dutch *Ere Divisie*, as they call their First Division, are in debt.

In fact, many small town teams have for years been forced to sell their best players every year in order to balance their books. The best example is FC Twente, who play at Enschede, a small town in north-west Holland close to the German border.

They transferred the Dutch stars Arnold Muhren and Frans Thijssen to Ipswich Town and have had to sell two or three players regularly every season. Amongst the stars transferred by them earlier were the Van der Kerkhoff twins, René and Willy, who were sold together to PSV Eindhoven.

Even the big city clubs are suffering. Feyenoord in Rotterdam and Ajax in Amsterdam, struggle to make ends meet for the fans will not pay to see them unless they are top of the league and meeting good opponents. So while both these sides could pull in capacity crowds of more than 60,000 for quite a few years they have fallen on hard times. The fans stay away from Feyenoord games

OPPOSITE Alfredo Di Stefano, the legendary centre forward of the great Real Madrid, now the manager of his old club. As a player Di Stefano was the top league scorer in Spain – five times.

against lowly clubs and Ajax fare no better. Only when the two crack clubs meet do they regularly pull in big crowds in both Amsterdam and Rotterdam, and generally the two former ace clubs are now suffering, though not as badly as the less well known clubs in the Dutch top flight. But there is a real crisis situation in Dutch football now, and no easy solution in sight.

While the Dutch were real amateurs, no one kept any comprehensive records. The official records show for example that in the 1946–47 season, Ajax were the champions, but played only ten games. PSV Eindhoven, the official champions in 1950–51, played eight matches and Willem II (Tilburg) won the title in season 1954–55, having played only six games. And no one knows who the leading scorers were, or whether they were ever published anywhere.

At that time the Dutch staged regional competitions and the winners of the various regional leagues played off for the championship at the end of the season under different formulas.

Although complete records are very hard to come by in some countries, there are others where FA officials have worked very hard to preserve their full records for posterity. Spain and Czechoslovakia are two excellent examples.

In Spain they published in 1956 an official FA annual that even showed every Spanish team line-up for every international match going back to 1920 and the players who helped win the FA Cup as far back as 1902.

For Spain I have also been able to obtain a full league table for the *Primera Division* for every season since the national league began in season 1928–29.

I also have a book entitled '60 Let Ceskoslovenske Kopane' . . . Sixty Years of Czech Football, published in 1961, which gives very detailed information on every aspect of their game. It includes a section of all their international line-ups going back to their first representative match, a Prague XI drawing 2–2 away to a Vienna XI in 1899.

The Italians also have an excellent annual publication with full league tables and results going back to season 1929–30 when their national league began. But many countries have completely neglected to keep records, and the result, in many countries is chaos. One of the worst is Turkey, where it appears that hardly anyone knows anything!

The championship tables for Italy clearly show the development of their awful defensive system *catenaccio*, which has been copied in some form or another by almost every country. Only the British have so far rejected the use of a *libero*, the Italian word for the player who stands free behind the line of three or four tight-marking defenders.

Valentino Mazzola of Torino, the top league scorer in 1946–47, is in fact the father of Sandro Mazzola who starred later for Internazionale-Milan. Valentino was one of the players of *Il Grande Torino* that scored 125 goals in 40 league matches in season 1947–48. A year later he, and all but one of the Torino players, died in the air crash at Superga. The plane carrying the team and reserves and officials back from a Latin Cup match, crashed into a monastery on a hill, outside Turin, in bad weather.

OPPOSITE Kevin Keegan who was the top scorer in English league games last season with 26 goals.

The Latin Cup was an annual competiton, abandoned with the coming of the

European Cup, but one of its forefathers and competed for at the end of every season by the champions of the four Latin countries, Spain, Italy, Portugal and France.

However, to return to the development of *catenaccio*, it has been said by many who should know better that it was invented by Helenio Herrera. In fact, the development can be seen ten years before HH arrived from Barcelona in the 1960's.

For example, Torino's goals tally of 125 was the highest post-war total but it soon began to decline, and by season 1952–53, Internazionale (Milano), better known in some countries as Inter-Milan, but known to the Italians simply as Inter, took the championship by scoring only 46 goals and conceding 24 in their 34 league matches. *Catenaccio* had been firmly established.

The results can be seen quite clearly as the years pass, but in fact it began in the 1950's and was developed by the smaller clubs who could not afford to import the big stars. With players like John Hansen from Denmark and Sweden's Gunnar Nordahl scoring freely, there were some big scores in league matches.

To counter the super-stars, someone dreamed up the idea of double-marking the opponent's star goal-getter—playing two men on him. That later led to the *libero*, and step by step to the system now hated by everyone who really likes football.

In fact the Nordahl who tops the scorers list in Sweden for three consecutive seasons between 1945 and 1948 was Gunnar Nordahl. One of three brothers who played for IFK Norrkoping, he impressed Italian scouts who saw him play in the 1948 Olympic Games soccer tournament in London and he joined AC Milan and became top scorer in Italy too. Later he continued to score goals for AS Roma, but was never the top marksman again after leaving AC Milan.

Another free scoring player was Jozef Bican, known to Czech fans as 'Pepi'. He spent most of his career with Slavia SK in Prague, but was capped for both Austria and Czechoslovakia. After being the leading scorer for Slavia for several seasons, they thought he was finished and transferred him to another Prague club, Vitkovice. Two years later he was again the leading goalscorer in Czechoslovakia, with his new club.

I was told a great story about 'Pepi' Bican while in Prague some years ago. Near the end of his career the FA selectors of the national team decided he was past his best and omitted him from the team for a match against Austria. Upset, and with league games cancelled to allow the national team time to prepare, 'Pepi' got a friend with a car to drop him off with his girlfriend at his country cottage, deep in the Bohemian pine forest, ten days before the big match. They took with them ample food and crates of beer.

Bican tried to forget his disappointment, but on the morning of the match he decided that he must at least go and wish his old colleagues luck, and see the game. But first he had to walk more than seven miles through the forest to reach the spot on the outskirts of Prague, where the tram lines began.

Arriving at Letna, the Sparta ground where the match was staged, Bican had

OPPOSITE Piero Prati, one of the best post-war strikers A.C. Milan have had, and the top league marksman in Italy in season 1967–68

a beer or two and some sausage and bread, and then strolled along to the main entrance to the ground. 'Any chance of a ticket?' he asked the gate-man who recognised him at once.

'Where have you been?' was the reply. 'You are playing'.

The Czech team had to be changed when one of the other stars received an injury in training, but no one could find Bican. They had even persuaded the authorities to ask him to contact the FA at the end of news bulletins on the radio, but Bican had no radio in his country cottage.

Bican went to the Czech dressing room at once, changed, played, and scored three goals after pre-match preparations that would give modern managers a nightmare.

The FA Cup Final scores also require some explanation. Many finals have ended in draws and in some continental countries, after extra time has failed to separate the two teams, they settle the result with penalty kicks. Where this has occurred, the winners are marked with an asterisk after their name.

Some finals, like that in Portugal in season 1951–52, really did end with a 5–4 scoreline after ninety minutes. But many more seem unusually high scores and some were settled over two legs, at home and away. In these cases the aggregate scores are given.

In some cases however, the finals have been drawn re-played, sometimes even going to two or three re-plays, and here the total scores are given.

In many continental countries the Football Association found it difficult to persuade either their clubs or the fans to accept a knock-out competition. In some countries, a few of the big clubs refused to take part in the FA Cup, and in many cases, even the final ties were very poorly supported.

Many continental officials looked enviously at England and Scotland where, since the earliest years of their Cup competitions, the finals have attracted huge crowds with the FA receiving a slice of the profits that has helped develop and pay for, the administration of the game.

In Poland their FA introduced the FA Cup in the early years but it was abandoned due to lack of interest. The cup was not competed for between 1926 and 1950. Then the Polish FA tried again, staging the Cup competition in 1950–51 and 1951–52 but were persuaded against it.

Similar results were experienced in many other countries, but the introduction of the European Cupwinners Cup gave everyone an extra incentive. Once it was realised that European competitions pulled big crowds, it was finally accepted everywhere though in some countries the final of the FA Cup still attracts only small crowds.

For Italy however, only the winners have been shown. This is because in most seasons there is no real final. At the moment the FA Cup is limited to clubs in the top two Divisions, Serie A and Serie B. They are divided into mini-leagues, playing off at home and away with the group winners going forward. Very often the first stage has been played off before the start of the league championship and then resumed in May or June. But even then, more often than not, the quarter finalists have been divided again into mini-leagues to

OPPOSITE Ion Ionescu who was twice the leading league goal scorer in Romania for his club, Rapid (Bucharest).

provide more fixtures, and the final pool has varied in size with the winners of the final mini-league being declared the winner.

This formula was once used in the seventies in Hungary and for that season there is no final score, only the winners, Diosgyor, who won the final pool.

Only the Spaniards have really accepted the idea of an FA Cup. Like everywhere else their game developed with regional leagues, and in the early years they began to stage an annual play-off amongst the winners of the regional leagues for the 'championship'.

Though the league system has been long established now in Spain, the FA Cup is still regarded in many quarters as the real championship, but the Spaniards are unique in this respect amongst continentals.

A few words about the West German tables will no doubt be of interest, particularly to those who do not follow the game abroad closely. Until 1963 the Germans based their game on regional competitions, according to geography. Thus, after the war they had leagues in the West, South, South-west and North, as well as a smaller league in West Berlin.

Then the top two teams from each *Regional-Liga* were qualified for the final play-offs and divided into two groups to play home and away games in mini-leagues. The winners of these two little competitions then met in what the Germans called the *Endspiel*.

So until the coming of the *Bundesliga* there was no truly national league in Germany, pre-war or post-war. And when the national league was formed it was falsely regarded in some quarters as a super-league for which many in England have long campaigned.

In fact, while a 16 club Division One would be good for the English game, and perhaps will come in time, the *Bundesliga* is nothing more than a truly national First Division.

Another interesting point concerns the German FA's choice of clubs for places in the *Bundesliga*. Places were awarded to clubs according to their past successes, playing strength, ground capacity and other facilities, and their financial position.

There was no place for either FC Bayern München or Borussia Mönchengladbach, who had to earn promotion. Then of course they went on to become two of the leading clubs in Europe and provided most of the players for the West German successes in the 1972 European Championship (for national teams), and the 1974 World Cup.

Between them these two clubs produced stars like Franz Beckenbauer and Gunter Netzer; Berti Vogts, Paul Breitner and the goal-scoring machine, Gerd Müller, known to his fans as 'Der Bomber'.

In fact, Müller never had a big shot as his tag implies, and never even tried long range shots of real power as Eusebio for example, did briefly in Portugal. Müller's talents were not unlike those of England's Jimmy Greaves. They both had the instinct that carried them into the right place at the right time.

Many of Müller's goals were what his national team manager, Helmut Schön, described as 'little-goals'. He was good in the air and excellent at

OPPOSITE Wlodzimierz Lubanski (Dark shirt), of Gornik Zabrze who played a big part in establishing Poland as a soccer power and was his country's top league scorer four years in a row in the sixties.

getting away from markers in the penalty area, with feints and quick sprints, but he developed one very good habit. Whenever he shot at goal, he would never stand, hands on hips, admiring his shot, which some players do. After shooting or heading at goal, Müller would follow up his first effort, and also followed up when colleagues made goal attempts. The result was that Müller found himself scoring from many little tap-in goals when the opposing goalkeeper fumbled the ball or when it re-bounded into play from a post or the cross-bar.

To return to the championship statistics, many countries have continually changed the number of clubs in their First Division. In some cases it has grown larger in what were comparatively underdeveloped countries before the Second World War.

One of the best examples of this is provided by Romania. They did not resume their national league after the war until season 1947–48 and began with a 26 match programme. Then it was increased to 30 matches, but returned to 26 before the 1950 spring to autumn campaign when they played only 22 games.

Then it varied almost haphazardly with 26, 24 and 22 games before it settled down again at 14 clubs (26 matches) in season 1960–61. In 1968 two more clubs were added and finally for the 1973–74 campaign there were 18 clubs in the top flight giving a league programme of 34 matches.

Similar changes have been made in many countries where the game has only reached a high standard quite recently, to give more matches and an increased income from gate receipts.

The Austrians went one step further after changing the number of their clubs several times. Because many of the smaller clubs could not keep going financially and compete with the old-established big clubs, it was decided in the seventies to have a ten club *Bundesliga* in which each club played everyone else four times—as they do in Scotland.

Italy, as an old-established football country, have moved the other way. They resumed, after the war with a 40 match league programme but by season 1948–49 it was down to a regular 38 matches (20 clubs). Then for many years it came down to 18 clubs before settling at 16 clubs to give a 30 match league programme as it is now.

The Italians have reduced their Serie A, as they know their First Division, for two major reasons. First, the development of the three European competitions for clubs has meant that a club doing well in Europe has a very hectic time. Secondly, the Italians have blank weekends to give their national team adequate time to prepare for international games.

The Italians have never played a competitive international match without at least ten days training and playing together.

We saw last season how hectic it became for Tottenham Hotspur and in the final weeks of the season they had a terrible time fitting in all their matches. In addition to their basic 42 league match programme they won the FA Cup (after a re-play), and also reached the final of the Football League Cup. They had a very good season in the First Division but would surely have done even better in a

OPPOSITE Kenny Dalglish who, with Glasgow Celtic was the top league scorer in Scotland in season 1975–76 and has since become the key man in the Liverpool attack.

smaller league, for they also had a good run in the European Cupwinners Cup.

A First Division with 16 clubs would perhaps be ideal, though there is no reason why there should not be 22 teams in the Second Division. And the Third and Fourth Divisions should be regionalised, and, as in all other countries, they should use part-time professional players in the lower Divisions.

Economics will eventually force changes but at the moment officials and many clubs are against change, and it may not come for some time.

There has, for many years, also been the argument about summer football. My personal feeling is that it would be of benefit, for the weather is the decisive factor. Shirt-sleeved crowds watching mid-week league games in June and July would certainly be bigger than those that freeze in the snow and cold of winter, and playing on an ice-bound pitch can be no pleasure for the players. It is one thing for clubs that can afford under-soil heating but numerically the vast majority of British players are amateurs who play on grounds with only the bare minimum of refinements and facilities.

British players, unaccustomed to ideal playing surfaces, will never match the best of the South Americans for skill as long as they continue to plough through mud and water, snow and ice.

If pitches are too hard in summer this can be adjusted by just the right amount of water spread on the pitch to provide a perfect playing surface for every game. But it is impossible to provide a good surface in the worst of the winter weather.

The Hungarians have often changed their season, though no one in Europe has yet moved their season to summer only, apart from the Scandinavian countries and the Soviet Union. In these countries they have such severe winters that football is absolutely impossible.

But even in Central Europe, where they have always had a winter break for three months it is sometimes impossible to know when the weather will strike. I have personally encountered snow and ice while driving abroad to watch football as early as November and as late as April.

In Hungary they began their season British style after the last war but then in 1950 they played only one round of matches in a 15 game half-season, staged in the autumn, in order to change. Then they played for a while as the Scandinavians do, starting in the spring and finishing the campaign in the autumn.

But the European Cup brought problems, for their champions could not take part until a year after they had won the title, and they changed their minds quite often. This accounts for the relatively small number of matches played in seasons 1950, 1957, 1963 and 1970, in order to make the change.

The Hungarian figures also show Ferenc Puskas the top league goalscorer with fifty goals for Kispest. This club was then adopted by the Hungarian army and renamed Honved, so that it is the same Puskas who topped the scorers list later for Honved.

Later still, Puskas was also the leading scorer in Spain on four occasions, as older readers will perhaps know, starring for Real Madrid.

OPPOSITE Gianni Rivera (Dark shirt), of A.C. Milan, who was equal top scorer in Italy in season 1972–73 when A.C. Milan won the Italian F.A. Cup.

AUSTRIA

Season	Champion club	P	W	D	L	F. A.	Pts.	Leading League Goalscorer		FA Cup Final			
1945–46	SC Rapid	22	16	3	3	99.24	35	Stojaspal (FK Austria)	34	SC Rapid	2	1st Vienna FC	1
1946–47	SC Wacker	20	14	2	4	61.24	30	Stojaspal (FK Austria)	18	SC Wacker	4	FK Austria	3
1947–48	SC Rapid	18	13	2	3	55.23	28	Stojaspal (FK Austria)	24	FK Austria	2	Sturm Graz	0
1948–49	FK Austria	18	13	1	4	65.27	27	Habitzl (Admira Vienna)	23	FK Austria	5	Vorwärts Steyr	2
1949–50	FK Austria	24	18	2	4	92.37	38	Decker (1st Vienna FC)	23	No competition			
1950–51	SC Rapid	24	20	3	1	133.40	43	Dienst (SC Rapid)	36	No competition			
1951–52	SC Rapid	26	20	1	5	107.38	41	Stojaspal (FK Austria)	31	No competition			
1952–53	FK Austria	26	21	3	2	106.38	45	Dienst (SC Rapid) Stojaspal (FK Austria)	30	No competition			
1953–54	SC Rapid	26	18	5	3	96.43	41	Dienst (SC Rapid)	25	No competition			
1954–55	1st Vienna FC	26	17	5	4	64.26	39	Brousek (SC Wacker)	31	No competition			
1955–56	SC Rapid	26	20	3	3	93.37	43	Buzek (1st Vienna FC)	33	No competition			
1956–57	SC Rapid	26	19	2	5	100.43	40	Dienst (SC Rapid)	32	No competition			
1957–58	Wiener Sport Klub	26	20	5	1	100.35	45	Horak (Wiener Sport Klub)	34				
1958–59	Wiener Sport Klub	26	20	6	0	104.35	46	Hof (Wiener Sport Klub)	32	Wiener AC	2	SC Rapid	0
1959–60	SC Rapid	26	18	6	2	87.32	42	Cejka (Wiener AC)	28	FK Austria	4	SC Rapid	2
1960–61	FK Austria	26	17	5	4	68.31	39	Nemec (FK Austria)	31	SC Rapid	3	1st Vienna	1
1961–62	FK Austria	26	19	4	3	65.23	42	Nemec (FK Austria)	24	FK Austria	4	Grazer AK	1
1962–63	FK Austria	26	17	4	5	60.26	38	Hof (Wiener Sport Klub)	21	FK Austria	1	Linzer ASK	0
1963–64	SC Rapid	26	19	5	2	69.27	43	Nemec (FK Austria)	20	Admira Vienna	1	FK Austria	0
1964–65	Linzer ASK	26	14	8	4	49.29	36	Gayer (Wiener Sport Klub)	18	Linzer ASK	2	Wiener Neustadt SC	1
1965–66	Admira Vienna	26	18	7	1	51.17	43	Buzek (FK Austria)	17	Admira Vienna	1	SC Rapid	0
1966–67	SC Rapid	26	20	1	5	72.29	41	Starek (SC Rapid)	21	FK Austria*	2	Linzer ASK	2
1967–68	SC Rapid	26	21	2	3	75.24	44	Bjerregaard (SC Rapid)	23	SC Rapid	2	Grazer AK	0
1968–69	FK Austria	28	19	8	1	80.35	46	Kögleberger (FK Austria)	31	SC Rapid	2	Wiener Sport Klub	1
1969–70	FK Austria	30	19	7	4	63.31	45	Kaltenbrunner (SC Rapid)	22	Wacker Innsbruck	1	Linzer ASK	0
1970–71	Wacker Innsbruck	30	20	4	6	68.30	44	Kreuz (Admira Vienna)	26	FK Austria	2	SC Rapid	1
1971–72	Wacker Innsbruck	28	15	9	4	49.20	39	Riedl (FK Austria)	16	SC Rapid	4	Wiener Sport Klub	3
1972–73	Wacker Innsbruck	30	18	7	5	57.25	43	Breuer (Wacker Innsbruck)	22	Wacker Innsbruck*	2	SC Rapid	2
1973–74	VOEST Linz	32	18	11	3	51.28	47	Krankl (SC Rapid)	36	FK Austria	3	FK Austria (Salzburg)	2
1974–75	Swarowski-Wacker Innsbruck	36	24	3	9	76.36	51	Kögleberger (FK Austria)	22	Swarowski-Wacker Innsbruck	3	Sturm Graz	2
1975–76	FK Austria	36	21	10	5	77.29	51	Pirkner (FK Austria)	21	SC Rapid*	2	Swarowski-Wacker Innsbruck	2
1976–77	Swarowski-Wacker Innsbruck	36	21	11	4	51.22	53	Krankl (SC Rapid)	32	FK Austria	4	Wiener Sport Klub	0
1977–78	FK Austria	36	23	10	3	77.34	56	Krankl (SC Rapid)	41	Swarowski-Wacker Innsbruck	3	VOEST Linz	2
1978–79	FK Austria	36	25	5	6	88.44	55	Schachner (FK Austria)	24	Swarowski-Wacker Innsbruck	2	Admira Vienna	1

World Cup Gallery

Season	Champion club	P	W	D	L	F.	A.	Pts	Leading League Goalscorer		FA Cup Final			
1979–80	FK Austria	36	20	10	6	84.	39	50	Schachner (FK Austria)	34	FK Austria	2	Casino Salzburg	1
1980–81	FK Austria	36	20	6	10	77.	46	46	Jurtin (Sturm Graz)	20	Grazer AK	2	Casino Salzburg	1
1981–82	SC Rapid	36	18	11	7	69.	43	47	Bakota (Sturm-Graz)	24	FK Austria	4	Swarowski-Wacker Innsbruck	1

LUIZINHO (Brazil)

BELGIUM

Season	Champion club	P	W	D	L	F. A.	Pts.	Leading League Goalscorer		FA Cup Final			
1945–46	FC Malines	36	22	11	3	112.41	55						
1946–47	RSC Anderlecht	36	21	8	7	108.37	50						
1947–48	FC Malines	30	19	5	6	96.42	43	Mermans (RSC Anderlecht)	23				
1948–49	RSC Anderlecht	30	18	5	7	91.38	41	Mermans (RSC Anderlecht)	28	No competition			
1949–50	RSC Anderlecht	30	19	7	4	92.32	45	Mermans (RSC Anderlecht)	37				
1950–51	RSC Anderlecht	30	16	6	8	78.35	38	De Herdt (Berchem)	27				
1951–52	Royal FC Liege	30	18	8	4	85.38	44	Coppens (Beerschot AC)	23				
1952–53	Royal FC Liege	30	18	6	6	79.40	42	Coppens (Beerschot AC)	33				
1953–54	RSC Anderlecht	30	15	7	8	82.34	37	Van den Bosch (RSC Anderlecht)	28	Standard Liege	3	Lierse S.K.	0
1954–55	RSC Anderlecht	30	17	7	6	85.31	41	Coppens (Beerschot AC)	34	Royal FC Antwerp	4	Waterschei Thor	0
1955–56	RSC Anderlecht	30	18	6	6	83.36	42	Mathonet (Standard Liege)	28	RRC Tournai	2	La Gantoise	1
1956–57	Royal FC Antwerp	30	19	8	3	69.28	46	Willems (ARA Gantoise)	34				
1957–58	Standard Liege	30	17	10	3	75.31	44	Van Gool (Royal FC Antwerp) Vliers (Beerschot AC)	24				
1958–59	RSC Anderlecht	30	19	6	5	72.23	44	Wegria (Royal FC Liege)	26	No competition			
1959–60	Lierse S.K.	30	16	6	8	57.40	38	Wegria (Royal FC Liege)	21				
1960–61	Standard Liege	30	18	9	3	67.25	45	Wegria (Royal FC Liege)	23				
1961–62	RSC Anderlecht	30	23	3	4	78.29	49	Stockman (RSC Anderlecht)	29				
1962–63	Standard Liege	30	19	8	3	71.26	46	Wegria (Royal FC Liege)	24				
1963–64	RSC Anderlecht	30	18	9	3	77.28	45	Van Himst (RSC Anderlecht)	26	La Gantoise	4	FC Diest	2
1964–65	RSC Anderlecht	30	24	3	3	87.22	51	Colonval (Tilleur)	25	RSC Anderlecht	3	Standard Liege	2
1965–66	RSC Anderlecht	30	21	5	4	88.18	47	Van Himst (RSC Anderlecht)	24	Standard Liege	1	RSC Anderlecht	0
1966–67	RSC Anderlecht	30	20	7	3	63.12	47	Mulder (RSC Anderlecht)	20	Standard Liege	3	Racing Malines	1
1967–68	RSC Anderlecht	30	20	6	4	67.24	46	Claessen (Standard Liege)	21	FC Bruges*	1	Beerschot AC	1
1968–69	Standard Liege	30	19	7	4	62.18	45	Nagy (Standard Liege)	20	Lierse S.K.	2	Racing-White FC	0
1969–70	Standard Liege	30	22	5	3	64.24	49	Emmerich (Beerschot AC)	29	FC Bruges	6	Daring CB	1
1970–71	Standard Liege	30	21	5	4	66.24	47	Kostedde (Standard Liege)	26	Beerschot AC	2	VV St. Trond	1
1971–72	RSC Anderlecht	30	19	7	4	66.25	45	Lambert (FC Bruges)	17	RSC Anderlecht	1	Standard Liege	0
1972–73	FC Bruges	30	17	11	2	53.26	45	Rensenbrink (RSC Anderlecht)	16	RSC Anderlecht	2	Standard Liege	1
1973–74	RSC Anderlecht	30	17	7	6	72.38	41	Ladinski (RSC Anderlecht)	22	KSV Waregem	4	FC Tongeren	1
1974–75	RWDM Molenbeek	38	25	11	2	92.39	61	Riedl (Royal FC Antwerp)	28	RSC Anderlecht	1	Royal FC Antwerp	0
1975–76	FC Bruges	36	22	8	6	81.38	52	Posthumus (Lierse S.K.)	26	RSC Anderlecht	4	Lierse S.K.	0
1976–77	FC Bruges	34	23	6	5	72.30	52	Van der Elst (RSC Anderlecht)	21	FC Bruges	4	RSC Anderlecht	3
1977–78	FC Bruges	34	22	7	5	73.48	51	Nickel (Standard Liege)	22	Beveren	2	Sporting Charleroi	0
1978–79	Beveren	34	19	11	4	62.24	49	Albert (Beveren)	28	Beerschot AC	1	FC Bruges	0
1979–80	FC Bruges	34	23	6	5	74.32	52	Vandenbergh (Lierse S.K.)	39	Waterschei (Genk)	2	Beveren	1
1980–81	RSC Anderlecht	34	26	5	3	83.24	57	Vandenbergh (Lierse S.K.)	24	Standard Liege	4	KSC Lokeren	0
1981–82	Standard Liege	34	19	10	5	59.28	48	Vandenbergh (Lierse S.K.)	25	Waterschei (Genk)	2	KSV Waregem	0

FALCAÕ (Brazil)

BULGARIA

Season	Champion club	P	W	D	L	F. A.	Pts.	Leading League Goalscorer		FA Cup Final			
1945–46										Levski-Spartak	4	Chernolometz Popovo	1
1946–47		No competition								Levski-Spartak	1	Botev Plovdiv	0
1947–48										Lokomotive Sofia	1	Lokomotive Plovdiv	0
1948–49	Levski-Spartak	18	15	3	0	48.8	33	Nedev (Cernomore Varna) Milanov (CSKA)	11	Levski-Spartak	2	CSKA	1
1950	Levski-Spartak	18	12	5	1	36.12	29	Hranov (Levski-Spartak)	11	Levski-Spartak	1	CSKA	0
1951	CSKA	22	18	1	3	62. 7	37	Milanov (CSKA)	13	CSKA	1	Akademik Sofia	0
1952	CSKA	22	13	7	2	38.12	33	Isakov (Slavia Sofia) Tashkov (Spartak Sofia)	10	Slavia Sofia	3	Spartak Sofia	1
1953	Levski-Spartak	28	19	5	4	48.22	43	Minchev (Spartak Pleven)	15	Lokomotive Sofia	2	Levski-Spartak	1
1954	CSKA	26	20	5	1	76.14	45	Tashkov (Slavia Sofia)	25	CSKA	2	Slavia Sofia	1
1955	CSKA	26	14	9	3	38.16	37	Diev (Spartak Plovdiv)	13	CSKA	5	Spartak Plovdiv	2
1956	CSKA	22	11	9	2	46.25	31	Vladimirov (Mineur Pernik)	16	Levski-Spartak	5	Botev Plovdiv	2
1957	CSKA	22	15	4	3	53.16	34	Iliev (Levski-Spartak)	14	Levski-Spartak	2	Spartak Plovdiv	1
1958	CSKA	11	7	4	0	19.9	18	Tashkov (Slavia Sofia) Arnavdov (Spartak Varna)	9	Spartak Plovdiv	1	Mineur Pernik	0
1958–59	CSKA	22	13	6	3	37.16	32	Vasilev (Slavia Sofia)	13	Levski-Spartak	1	Spartak Plovdiv	0
1959–60	CSKA	22	12	8	2	42.18	32	Yordanov (Levski-Spartak) Kostov (Spartak Varna)	12	Septemvri Sofia	4	Lokomotive Plovdiv	3
1960–61	CSKA	26	18	4	4	56.17	40	Sotirov (Botev Plovdiv)	20	CSKA	3	Spartak Varna	0
1961–62	CSKA	26	18	5	3	60.25	41	Yordanov (Dunav Ruse)	23	Botev Plovdiv	3	Dunav Ruse	0
1962–63	Spartak Plovdiv	30	19	5	6	57.33	43	Diev (Spartak Plovdiv)	26	Slavia Sofia	2	Botev Plovdiv	0
1963–64	Lokomotive Sofia	30	18	8	4	53.28	44	Zanev (CSKA)	26	Slavia Sofia	3	Botev Plovdiv	2
1964–65	Levski-Spartak	30	18	6	6	59.28	42	Asparoukhov (Levski-Spartak)	27	CSKA	3	Levski-Spartak	2
1965–66	CSKA	30	17	8	5	53.30	42	Spasov (Marek	21	Slavia Sofia	1	CSKA	0
1966–67	Botev Plovdiv	30	13	12	5	39.24	38	Jekov (Beroe)	21	Levski-Spartak	3	Spartak Sofia	0
1967–68	Levski-Spartak	30	18	9	3	61.29	45	Jekov (Beroe)	31	Spartak Sofia	3	Beroe	2
1969	CSKA	30	22	3	5	74.38	47	Jekov (CSKA)	36	CSKA	2	Levski-Spartak	1
1969–70	Levski-Spartak	30	23	4	3	67.17	50	Jekov (CSKA)	31	Levski-Spartak	2	CSKA	1
1970–71	CSKA	30	21	6	3	74.21	48	Yakimov (CSKA)	26	Levski-Spartak	3	Lokomotive Plovdiv	0
1971–72	CSKA	34	26	6	2	95.28	58	Jekov (CSKA)	27	CSKA	3	Slavia Sofia	0
1972–73	CSKA	34	22	7	5	80.40	51	Jekov (CSKA)	29	CSKA	2	Beroe	1
1973–74	Levski-Spartak	30	21	5	4	58.30	47	Petkov (Beroe)	20	CSKA	2	Levski-Spartak	1
1974–75	CSKA	30	15	9	6	52.32	39	Pritargov (Trakia Plovdiv)	20	Slavia Sofia	3	Lokomotive Sofia	2
1975–76	CSKA	30	17	9	4	61.30	43	Petkov (Beroe)	19	Levski-Spartak	4	CSKA	3
1976–77	Levski-Spartak	30	16	11	3	73.34	43	Panov (Levski-Spartak)	20	Levski-Spartak	2	Lokomotive Sofia	1
1977–78	Lokomotive Sofia	30	16	10	4	40.16	42	Mladenov (Beroe)	21	Marek	1	CSKA	0
1978–79	Levski-Spartak	30	18	7	5	54.29	43	Gochev (Levski-Spartak)	19	Levski-Spartak	4	Beroe	1
1979–80	CSKA	30	18	10	2	60.30	46	Djevizov (CSKA)	21	Slavia Sofia	3	Beroe	1

Season	Champion club	P	W	D	L	F.	A.	Pts	Leading League Goalscorer		FA Cup Final			
1980–81	CSKA	30	14	12	4	70	32	40	Slavkov (Trakia)	31	Trakia Plovdiv	1	Pirin (Blagoevgrad)	0
1981–82	CSKA	30	22	3	5	73	27	47	Valtchev (Levski-Spartak)	24	Lokomotive Sofia	2	Lokomotive Plovdiv	1

SAAD AL-HOUTI (Kuwait)

CZECHOSLOVAKIA

Season	Champion club	P	W	D	L	F. A.	Pts.	Leading League Goalscorer		FA Cup Final			
1945–46	AC Sparta	18	16	0	2	80.34	32	Bican (Slavia SK)	31	No Competition			
1946–47	Slavia SK	26	19	2	5	110.54	40	Bican (Slavia SK)	43				
1947–48	AC Sparta	20	12	3	5	62.35	27	Cejp (AC Sparta)	21				
1949	Slovan Bratislava	26	18	5	3	93.33	41	Hlavacek (Slavia SK)	28				
1950	Slovan Bratislava	26	16	3	7	62.35	35	Bican (Vitkovice ZKG)	22				
1951	Slovan Bratislava	26	14	5	7	58.36	33	Jaros (Union Teplice)	16				
1952	AC Sparta	26	18	5	3	63.22	41	Wiecek (Banik Ostrava)	20				
1953	Dukla Prague	13	10	2	1	41.12	22	Majer (SONP Kladno)	13				
1954	AC Sparta	22	13	4	5	45.21	30	Pesek (AC Sparta)	15				
1955	Slovan Bratislava	22	13	5	4	41.14	31	Pazicky (Slovan Bratislava)	19				
1956	Dukla Prague	22	12	8	2	57.20	32	Dvorak (Dukla Prague)	15				
1957–58	Dukla Prague	33	16	8	9	60.38	40	Wiecek (Banik Ostrava)	25				
1958–59	Inter-Bratislava	26	16	8	2	56.27	40	Wiecek (Banik Ostrava)	20				
1959–60	Spartak Hradec Kralove	26	13	8	5	43.27	34	Pucher (Slovan Nitra)	18				
1960–61	Dukla Prague	26	17	5	4	66.23	39	Kucera (Dukla Prague) Pavlovic (Tatran Presov)	17	Dukla Prague	3	Dynamo Zilina	0
1961–62	Dukla Prague	26	15	5	6	81.30	35	Scherer (Inter-Bratislava)	24	Slovan Bratislava	5	Dukla Prague	2
1962–63	Dukla Prague	26	16	3	7	49.25	35	Petros (Tatran Presov)	19	Slovan Bratislava	9	Slavia SK	0
1963–64	Dukla Prague	26	16	5	5	52.26	37	Pavlovic (Tatran Presov)	21	AC Sparta	4	VSS Kosice	1
1964–65	AC Sparta	26	18	6	2	59.22	42	Bencz (Jednota Trencin)	21	Dukla Prague*	0	Slovan Bratislava	0
1965–66	Dukla Prague	26	13	7	6	40.23	33	Michalik (Banik Ostrava)	15	Dukla Prague	6	Tatran Presov	1
1966–67	AC Sparta	26	18	3	5	53.21	39	Adamec (Spartak Trnava)	22	Spartak Tranava*	4	AC Sparta	4
1967–68	Spartak Trnava	26	15	5	6	57.26	35	Adamec (Spartak Tranva)	19	Slovan Bratislava	2	Dukla Prague	1
1968–69	Spartak Trnava	26	17	5	4	50.21	39	Petras (Dukla Banska Bystrica)	20	Dukla Prague	2	VCHZ Pardubice	1
1969–70	Slovan Bratislava	30	16	11	3	39.15	43	Adamec (Spartak Trnava)	16	TJ Gottwaldov*	3	Slovan Bratislava	3
1970–71	Spartak Trnava	30	17	6	7	52.27	40	Adamec (Spartak Trnava) Nehoda (TJ Gottwaldov)	16	Spartak Trnava	7	Skoda Plzen	2
1971–72	Spartak Trnava	30	17	10	3	60.25	44	Capkovic (Slovan Bratislava)	19	AC Sparta*	4	Slovan Bratislava	4
1972–73	Spartak Trnava	30	16	7	7	47.20	39	Jozsa (Lokomotiva Kosice)	21	Banik Ostrava	4	VSS Kosice	3
1973–74	Slovan Bratislava	30	15	7	8	58.39	37	Bicovsky (Teplice) Jozsa (Lokomotiva Kosice)	17	Slovan Bratislava*	1	Slavia SK	1
1974–75	Slovan Bratislava	30	16	7	7	72.34	39	Petras (Inter-Bratislava)	20	Spartak Trnava	4	AC Sparta	1
1975–76	Banik Ostrava	30	14	9	7	37.29	37	Gallis (VSS Kosice)	21	AC Sparta	4	Slovan Bratislava	2
1976–77	Dukla Prague	30	18	6	6	61.33	42	Jozsa (Lokomotiva Kosice)	18	Lokomotiva Kosice	2	Union Teplice	1
1977–78	Zbrojovka Brno	30	18	7	5	64.25	43	Kroupa (Zbrojovka Brno)	20	Banik Ostrava	1	Jednota Trencin	0
1978–79	Dukla Prague	30	18	5	7	65.24	41	Kroupa (Zbrojovka Brno) Nehoda (Dukla Prague)	17	Lokomotiva Kosice	2	Banik Ostrava	1
1979–80	Banik Ostrava	30	16	9	5	47.23	41	Licka (Banik Ostrava)	18	AC Sparta	2	ZTS Kosice	0

World Cup Gallery

WOODCOCK (England)

Season	Champion club	P	W	D	L	F.	A.	Pts	Leading League Goalscorer		FA Cup Final			
1980–81	Banik Ostrava	30	18	4	8	44.	19	40	Masny (Slovan Bratislava)	16	Dukla Prague	4	Dukla Banska Bystrica	1
1981–2	Dukla Prague	30	18	6	6	54.	20	42	Vizek (Dukla Prague) Herda (Slavia SK)	15	Slovan Bratislava*	0	Bohemians	0

DENMARK

Season	Champion club	P	W	D	L	F. A.	Pts.	Leading League Goalscorer		FA Cup Final			
1945–46	B.93 (Boldklubben 1893)	18	13	2	3	61.29	28	Hansen (K) (B.93)	12				
1946–47	A.B. (Akademisk Boldklub)	18	12	4	2	56.36	28	Ronvang (A.B.)	11				
1947–48	KB (Kjobenhavns Boldklub)	18	16	1	1	48.13	33	Hansen (J) (Frem)	13				
1948–49	KB	18	12	3	3	37.17	27	Hansen (K.A.) (A.B.)	11	No competition			
1949–50	KB	18	12	4	2	36.11	28	Sebach (A.B.)	12				
1950–51	A.B.	18	11	6	1	34.15	28	Lundberg (A.B.)	11				
1951–52	A.B.	18	12	2	4	40.21	26	Rechendorff (A.B.)	14				
1952–53	KB	18	14	2	2	43.25	30	Lyngsa (KB)	12				
1953–54	Koge	18	10	3	5	45.34	23	Christensen (AB)	12				
1954–55	AGF Aarhus	18	9	6	3	38.24	24	Keldberg (AGF Aarhus)	13	AGF Aarhus	4	IT Chang (Axalberg)	0
1955–56	AGF Aarhus	18	10	5	3	48.25	25	Nielsen (O.B.) (A.B.)	14	Frem (Copenhagen)	1	A.B.	0
1956–57	AGF Aarhus	22	18	3	1	55.31	39	Jensen (J) (AGF Aarhus)	19	AGF Aarhus	2	Esbjerg	0
1958	Vejle BK	22	12	6	4	66.32	30	Enoksen (Vejle BK)	20	Vejle BK	3	KB	2
1959	B.1909 Odense	22	14	5	3	47.28	33	Lerby (B.1903)	19	Vejle BK	2	AGF Aarhus	1
1960	AGF Aarhus	22	13	6	3	52.31	32	Nielsen (H) (Frem)	19	AGF Aarhus	2	Frem (Saxobing)	0
1961	Esbjerg	22	15	3	4	52.18	33	Ravn (J) (KB)	26	AGF Aarhus	2	KB	0
1962	Esbjerg	22	17	3	2	61.16	37	Enoksen (AGF Aarhus)	24	B.1909 (Odense)	1	Esbjerg	0
1963	Esbjerg	22	15	3	4	56.28	33	Haastrup (B.1909)	21	B.1913 (Odense)	2	Koge BK	1
1964	B.1909 Odense	22	14	5	3	47.28	33	Ravn (J) (KB)	21	Esbjerg	2	KFUM (Odense)	1
1965	Esbjerg	22	12	7	3	53.24	31	Bjerregard (J) (AGF Aarhus)	18	AGF Aarhus	1	KB	0
1966	Hvidovre	22	11	9	2	40.16	31	Enoksen (AGF Aarhus)	16	AGF Aarhus	3	KB	1
1967	A.B.	22	14	3	5	42.28	31	Nielsen (L) (Frem)	15	Randers Freja	1	A.B.	0
1968	KB	22	13	3	6	50.26	29	Holmstrom (KB)	23	Randers Freja	3	Vejle BK	1
1969	B.1903 (Copenhagen)	22	15	4	3	58.25	34	Forsing (O) (B.1903)	19	KB	3	Frem (Copenhagen)	0
1970	B.1903 (Copenhagen)	22	11	5	6	56.36	27	Forsing (O) (B.1903)	24	Aalborg BK	2	Lyngby (Copenhagen)	1
1971	Vejle BK	22	13	3	6	61.40	29	Brage (KB)	19	B.1909 (Odense)	1	Frem (Copenhagen)	0
1972	Vejle BK	22	16	1	5	65.33	33	Lund (K) (Vejle BK) Nielsen (J) (B.1901 Nykobing)	16	Vejle BK	2	Fremad (Amager)	0
1973	Hvidovre	22	10	7	5	52.33	27	Aabech (Hvidovre)	28	Randers Freja	2	B.1901 Nykobing	0
1974	KB	22	15	3	4	48.24	33	Holmstrom (KB)	24	Vanloese IF	5	Odense BK.1887	2
1975	Koge BK	30	17	7	6	61.31	41	Petersen (KB)	26	Vejle BK	1	Holbaek	0
1976	B.1903 (Copenhagen)	30	16	8	6	51.29	40	Jespersen (Aalborg BK)	22	Esbjerg	2	Holbaek	1
1977	Odense BK.1887	30	19	9	2	66.27	47	Hansen (A) (Odense BK.1887)	23	Vejle BK	2	B.1909 (Odense)	1
1978	Vejle BK	30	19	6	5	64.33	44	Eriksen (J) (Odense BK.1887)	22	Frem (Copenhagen)*	1	Esbjerg	1
1979	Esbjerg	30	18	10	2	55.30	46	Eriksen (J) (Odense BK.1887)	21	B.1903 (Copenhagen)	1	Koge BK	0
1980	KB	30	16	8	6	59.35	40	Aabech (KB)	19	Hvidovre	5	Lyngby (Copenhagen)	3
1981	Hvidovre	30	15	10	5	42.25	40	Hansen (A) (Odense BK.1887)	28	Vejle BK	2	Frem (Copenhagen)	1
1982										B.93 (Copenhagen)	4	B.1909 (Odense)	3

World Cup Gallery

SMOLAREK (Poland)

ENGLAND

Season	Champion club	P	W	D	L	F. A.	Pts.	Leading League Goalscorer		FA Cup Final			
1945–46		No competition								Derby County	4	Charlton Ath	1
1946–47	Liverpool	42	25	7	10	84.52	57	Westcott (Wolverhampton)	37	Charlton Ath	1	Burnley	0
1947–48	Arsenal	42	23	13	6	81.32	59	Rooke (Arsenal)	33	Manchester Utd	4	Blackpool	2
1948–49	Portsmouth	42	25	8	9	84.42	58	Moir (Bolton)	25	Wolverhampton	3	Leicester City	1
1949–50	Portsmouth	42	22	9	11	74.38	53	Davis (Sunderland)	25	Arsenal	2	Liverpool	0
1950–51	Tottenham	42	25	10	7	82.44	60	Mortensen (Blackpool)	30	Newcastle Utd	2	Blackpool	0
1951–52	Manchester Utd	42	23	11	8	95.52	57	Robledo (G) (Newcastle Utd)	33	Newcastle Utd	1	Arsenal	0
1952–53	Arsenal	42	21	12	9	97.64	54	Wayman (Preston)	24	Blackpool	4	Bolton	3
1953–54	Wolverhampton	42	25	7	10	96.56	57	Glazzard (Huddersfield)	29	West Brom	3	Preston	2
1954–55	Chelsea	42	20	12	10	81.57	52	Allen (West Brom)	27	Newcastle Utd	3	Manchester City	1
1955–56	Manchester Utd	42	25	10	7	83.51	60	Lofthouse (Bolton)	33	Manchester City	3	Birmingham City	1
1956–57	Manchester Utd	42	28	8	6	103.54	64	Charles (Leeds Utd)	38	Aston Villa	2	Manchester Utd	1
1957–58	Wolverhampton	42	28	8	6	103.47	64	Smith (Tottenham)	36	Bolton	2	Manchester Utd	0
1958–59	Wolverhampton	42	28	5	9	110.49	61	Greaves (Chelsea) Smith (Tottenham)	32	Notts Forest	2	Luton Town	1
1959–60	Burnley	42	24	7	11	85.61	55	Viollet (Manchester Utd)	32	Wolverhampton	3	Blackburn Rovers	0
1960–61	Tottenham	42	31	4	7	115.55	66	Greaves (Chelsea)	41	Tottenham	2	Leicester City	0
1961–62	Ipswich Town	42	24	8	10	93.67	56	Crawford (Ipswich) Kevan (West Brom)	33	Tottenham	3	Burnley	1
1962–63	Everton	42	25	11	6	84.42	61	Greaves (Tottenham)	37	Manchester Utd	3	Leicester City	1
1963–64	Liverpool	42	26	5	11	92.45	57	Greaves (Tottenham)	35	West Ham	3	Preston	2
1964–65	Manchester Utd	42	26	9	7	89.39	61	McEvoy (Blackburn) Greaves (Tottenham)	29	Liverpool	2	Leeds Utd	1
1965–66	Liverpool	42	26	9	7	79.34	61	Hunt (Liverpool)	30	Everton	3	Sheff Wed	2
1966–67	Manchester Utd	42	24	12	6	84.45	60	Davies (Southampton)	37	Tottenham	2	Chelsea	1
1967–68	Manchester City	42	26	6	10	86.43	58	Best (Manchester Utd) Davies (Southampton)	28	West Brom	1	Everton	0
1968–69	Leeds Utd	42	27	13	2	66.26	67	Greaves (Tottenham)	27	Manchester City	1	Leicester City	0
1969–70	Everton	42	29	8	5	72.34	66	Astle (West Brom)	25	Chelsea	4	Leeds Utd	3
1970–71	Arsenal	42	29	7	6	71.29	65	Brown (A) (West Brom)	28	Arsenal	2	Liverpool	1
1971–72	Derby County	42	24	10	8	69.33	58	Lee (Manchester City)	33	Leeds Utd	1	Arsenal	0
1972–73	Liverpool	42	25	10	7	72.42	60	Robson (West Ham)	28	Sunderland	1	Leeds Utd	0
1973–74	Leeds Utd	42	24	14	4	66.31	62	Channon (Southampton)	21	Liverpool	3	Newcastle Utd	0
1974–75	Derby County	42	21	11	10	67.49	53	Macdonald (Newcastle Utd)	21	West Ham	2	Fulham	0
1975–76	Liverpool	42	23	14	5	66.31	60	MacDougall (Norwich)	23	Southampton	1	Manchester Utd	0
1976–77	Liverpool	42	23	11	8	62.33	57	Gray (Aston Villa) Macdonald (Arsenal)	25	Manchester Utd	2	Liverpool	1
1977–78	Notts Forest	42	25	14	3	69.24	64	Latchford (Everton)	30	Ipswich Town	1	Arsenal	0
1978–79	Liverpool	42	30	8	4	85.16	68	Worthington (Bolton)	24	Arsenal	3	Manchester Utd	2

World Cup Gallery

Season	Champion club	P	W	D	L	F.	A.	Pts	Leading League Goalscorer		FA Cup Final			
1979–80	Liverpool	42	25	10	7	81	30	60	Boyer (Southampton)	23	West Ham	1	Arsenal	0
1980–81	Aston Villa	42	26	8	8	72	40	60	Archibald (Tottenham) Withe (Aston Villa)	20	Tottenham	4	Manchester City	3
1981–82	Liverpool	42	26	9	7	80	32	87	Keegan (Southampton)	26	Tottenham	2	Q.P.R.	1

URIBE (Peru)

FINLAND

Season	Champion club	P	W	D	L	F. A.	Pts.	Leading League Goalscorer		FA Cup Final			
1945–46										No competition			
1946–47		Two competitions											
1947–48													
1948	VPS Vaasa	15	11	2	2	41.12	24	Myntti (Vaasa IFK)	15				
1949	TPS Turku	22	15	4	3	53.25	34	Asikainen (Ilves, Tampere) Lintamo (VPS Vaasa)	20				
1950	Ilves, Tampere	18	10	5	3	38.17	25	Asikainen (Ilves, Tampere) Saarinen (VPS Vaasa)	15				
1951	KTP Kotka	18	10	7	1	44.26	27	Forsberg (Kiffen)	16				
1952	KTP Kotka	18	10	6	2	52.20	26	Vanhanen (KTP Kotka)	16				
1953	Vaasa IFK	18	10	4	4	40.23	24	Forss (Pyrkiva)	15				
1954	Pyrkiva (Turun)	18	10	6	2	42.20	26	Koskinen (TuTo)	16				
1955	HIFK Helsinki	18	9	7	2	36.19	25	Asikainen (Kiffen)	12	Valkeakosken Haka	5	HPS Helsinki	1
1956	KuPS Kuopio	18	11	5	2	31.12	27	Styck (HJK Helsinki)	20	P-Posat, Helsinki	2	TKT Tampere	1
1957	HPS Helsinki	18	11	4	3	49.27	26	Sundelin (TPS Turku)	21	Drott (Pietarsaari)	2	KPT Kuopio	1
1958	KuPS Kuopio	18	13	0	5	40.22	26	Pahlman (HPS Helsinki) Lehtovirta (TPS Turku)	17	KTP Kotka	4	HIFK Helsinki	1
1959	HIFK Helsinki	18	11	5	2	43.26	27	Sundelin (TPS Turku)	21	Valkeakosken Haka	2	HIFK Helsinki	1
1960	Valkeakosken Haka	22	20	1	1	78.23	41	Sundelin (TPS Turku)	30	Valkeakosken Haka	3	RU-38 Pori	1
1961	HIFK Helsinki	22	14	3	5	57.26	31	Pahlman (HPS Helsinki)	20	KTP Kotka	5	P-Posat, Helsinki	2
1962	Valkeakosken Haka	22	15	2	5	63.33	32	Österlund (HIFK Helsinki)	22	HPS Helsinki	5	RoPS Rovaniemi	0
1963	Reipas Lahti	22	13	6	3	44.18	32	Lyytikainen (HIFK Helsinki)	16	Valkeakosken Haka	1	Reipas Lahti	0
1964	HJK Helsinki	22	14	6	2	42.18	34	Tolsa (KTP Kotka)	26	Reipas Lahti	1	Lapa Lappeenranta	0
1965	Valkeakosken Haka	22	14	3	5	56.28	31	Pahlman (HJK Helsinki)	22	AIFK Turku	1	TPS Turku	0
1966	KuPS Kuopio	22	12	5	5	41.23	29	Hyvärinen (KuPS Kuopio)	16	HJK Helsinki	6	KTP Kotka	1
1967	Reipas Lahti	22	14	4	4	55.27	32	Lindholm (TPS Turku)	22	KTP Kotka	2	Reipas Lahti	0
1968	TPS Turku	22	14	4	4	48.19	32	Lindholm (TPS Turku)	22	KuPS Kuopio	2	KTP Kotka	1
1969	KPV Kokkola	22	17	1	4	44.13	35	Lamberg (KPV Kokkola) Talaslahti (HJK Helsinki)	18	Valkeakosken Haka	2	Honka (Tapiola)	0
1970	Reipas Lahti	22	14	4	4	45.28	32	Paatelainen (HIFK Helsinki)	22	MP Mikkeli	4	Reipas Lahti	1
1971	TPS Turku	26	13	8	5	53.25	34	Toivola (MP Mikkeli)	17	MP Mikkeli	4	VPS Vaasa	1
1972	TPS Turku	22	15	1	6	44.19	31	Paatelainen (HIFK Helsinki) Suhonen (TPS Turku)	16	Reipas Lahti	2	VPS Vaasa	0
1973	HJK Helsinki	22	13	5	4	36.21	31	Lamberg (KPV Kokkola)	13	Reipas Lahti	2	SePS (Seinajoki)	0
1974	KuPS Kuopio	22	13	7	2	62.30	33	Salo (TPS Turku)	17	Reipas Lahti	1	OTP Oulu	0
1975	TPS Turku	22	13	6	3	34.18	32	Rantanen (MP Mikkeli)	16	Reipas Lahti	6	HJK Helsinki	2
1976	KuPS Kuopio	22	13	6	3	40.21	32	Paatelainen (Valkeakosken Haka)	17	Reipas Lahti	2	Ilves, Tampere	0
1977	Valkeakosken Haka	22	15	3	4	43.15	33	Paatelainen (Valkeakosken Haka)	20	Valkeakosken Haka	3	SePS (Seinajoki)	1
1978	HJK Helsinki	22	13	7	2	52.29	33	Ismail (HJK Helsinki)	20	Reipas Lahti	4	KPT Kuopio	2

World Cup Gallery

Season	Champion club	P	W	D	L	F. A.	Pts	Leading League Goalscorer		FA Cup Final			
1979	OPS Oulu	22	11	10	1	39.15	32	Linnusmäki (Ilves, Tampere)	13	Ilves, Tampere	2	TPS Turku	0
1980	OPS Oulu	22	13	8	1	4915	34	Rajaniemi (SePsi-78)	14	KTP Kotka	3	Valkeakosken Haka	2
1981	HJK Helsinki	29	17	5	7	57.32	39	Himanka (OPS Oulu)	22	HJK Helsinki	4	Kuusysi (Lahti)	0

KUNDE (Cameroon)

FRANCE

Season	Champion club	P	W	D	L	F.	A.	Pts.	Leading League Goalscorer		FA Cup Final			
1945–46	Lille OSC	34	19	7	8	89	44	45	Bihel (Lille OSC)	28	Lille OSC	4	Red Star (Paris)	2
1946–47	Roubaix	38	24	5	9	71	47	53	Sinibaldi (Reims)	33	Lille OSC	2	RC Strasbourg	0
1947–48	Olympique Marseille	34	20	8	6	83	43	48	Baratte (Lille OSC)	31	Lille OSC	3	RC Lens	2
1948–49	Reims	34	22	4	8	90	54	48	Baratte (Lille OSC)	27	Racing Club de Paris	5	Lille OSC	2
1949–50	Girondins, Bordeaux	34	21	9	4	88	40	51	Grumellon (Stade Rennes)	25	Reims	2	Racing Club de Paris	0
1950–51	OGC Nice	34	18	5	11	73	46	41	Piantoni (FC Nancy)	28	RC Strasbourg	3	US Valenciennes	0
1951–52	OGC Nice	34	21	4	9	65	42	46	Andersson (Olympique Marseille)	31	OGC Nice	5	Girondins, Bordeaux	3
1952–53	Reims	34	22	4	8	86	36	48	Andersson (Olympique Marseille)	35	Lille OSC	2	FC Nancy	1
1953–54	Lille OSC	34	17	13	4	49	22	47	Kargu (Girondins, Bordeaux)	27	OGC Nice	2	Olympique Marseille	1
1954–55	Reims	34	19	6	9	78	53	44	Bliard (Reims)	30	Lille OSC	5	Girondins, Bordeaux	2
1955–56	OGC Nice	34	18	7	9	60	43	43	Cisowski (Racing Club de Paris)	31	UA Sedan	3	AS Troyes	1
1956–57	St. Etienne	34	20	9	5	88	45	49	Cisowski (Racing Club de Paris)	33	US Toulouse	6	SCO Angers	3
1957–58	Reims	34	22	4	8	89	42	48	Fontaine (Reims)	34	Reims	3	Olympique Nimes	1
1958–59	OGC Nice	38	24	8	6	80	38	56	Cisowski (Racing Club de Paris)	30	AS Le Havre	5	FC Sochaux	2
1959–60	Reims	38	26	8	4	109	46	60	Fontaine (Reims)	28	AS Monaco	4	St. Etienne	2
1960–61	AS Monaco	38	26	5	7	77	42	57	Piantoni (Reims)	28	UA Sedan	3	Olympique Nimes	1
1961–62	Reims	38	21	6	11	83	60	48	Sekou (Montpellier)	25	St. Etienne	1	FC Nancy	0
1962–63	AS Monaco	38	20	10	8	77	44	50	Masnaghetti (US Valenciennes)	35	AS Monaco	2	Olympique Lyon	0
1963–64	St. Etienne	34	18	8	8	71	47	44	Oudjani (RC Lens)	30	Olympique Lyon	2	Girondins, Bordeaux	0
1964–65	FC Nantes	34	16	11	7	66	45	43	Simon (FC Nantes)	24	Stade Rennes	5	UA Sedan	3
1965–66	FC Nantes	38	26	8	4	84	36	60	Gondet (FC Nantes)	36	RC Strasbourg	1	FC Nantes	0
1966–67	St. Etienne	38	24	6	8	82	37	54	Revelli (St. Etienne)	31	Olympique Lyon	3	FC Sochaux	1
1967–68	St. Etienne	38	24	9	5	78	30	57	Sansonetti (Ajaccio)	36	St. Etienne	2	Girondins, Bordeaux	1
1968–69	St. Etienne	34	24	5	5	70	26	53	Guy (Olympique Lyon)	25	Olympique Marseille	2	Girondins, Bordeaux	0
1969–70	St. Etienne	34	25	6	3	88	30	56	Revelli (St. Etienne)	28	St. Etienne	5	FC Nantes	0
1970–71	Olympique Marseille	38	23	9	6	94	48	55	Skoblar (Olympique Marseille)	44	Stade Rennes	1	Olympique Lyon	0
1971–72	Olympique Marseille	38	24	8	6	78	37	56	Skoblar (Olympique Marseille)	30	Olympique Marseille	2	SEC Bastia	1
1972–73	FC Nantes	38	23	9	6	67	31	55	Skoblar (Olympique Marseille)	26	Olympique Lyon	2	FC Nantes	1
1973–74	St. Etienne	38	23	9	6	74	40	55	Bianchi (Reims)	30	St. Etienne	2	AS Monaco	1
1974–75	St. Etienne	38	23	6	9	70	39	52	Onnis (AS Monaco)	30	St. Etienne	2	RC Lens	0
1975–76	St. Etienne	38	18	15	5	68	39	51	Bianchi (Reims)	34	Olympique Marseille	2	Olympique Lyon	0
1976–77	FC Nantes	38	25	8	5	80	40	58	Bianchi (Reims)	28	St. Etienne	2	Reims	1
1977–78	AS Monaco	38	22	9	7	79	46	53	Bianchi (Paris St. Germain)	37	FC Nancy	1	OGC Nice	0
1978–79	RC Strasbourg	38	22	12	4	68	28	56	Bianchi (Paris St. Germain)	27	FC Nantes	4	Auxerre	1
1979–80	FC Nantes	38	26	5	7	78	30	57	Kostedde (Laval) Onnis (AS Monaco)	21	AS Monaco	3	Orleans	1
1980–81	St. Etienne	38	23	11	4	68	26	57	Onnis (Tours)	24	SEC Bastia	2	St. Etienne	1
1981–82	AS Monaco	38	24	7	7	70	29	55	Onnis (Tours)	29	Paris St. Germain*	2	St. Etienne	2

SZARMACH (Poland)

GERMANY (EAST)

Season	Champion club		P	W	D	L	F.	A.	Pts	Leading League Goalscorer		FA Cup Final			
1945–46 / 1946–47	No competition														
1948	SG Planitz	1	Freiimfelde Halle						0						
1949	ZSG Halle	4	Fortuna Erfurt						1			Waggonbau Dessau	1	Geru Sud	0
	Oberliga Records		P	W	D	L	F.	A.	Pts						
1949–50	Horch Zwickau		26	20	1	5	69.	27	41	Werner (Dresden Friedrichstadt)	21	EHW Thale	4	KWU Erfurt	0
1950–51	Chemie Leipzig		34	22	6	6	66.	23	50	Schone (Rotation Babelsberg)	38	No competition			
1951–52	Turbine Halle		36	21	11	4	80.	42	53	Weissenfels (Lokomotive Stendal) / Krause (Chemie Leipzig)	27	Volkspolizei Dresden	3	Einheit Pankow	0
1952–53	Dynamo Dresden		32	15	8	9	51.	33	38	Arlt (Rotation Dresden)	26	No competition			
1953–54	Turbine Erfurt		28	17	5	6	58.	36	39	Satrapa (Wismut Karl-Marx-Stadt) / Vollrath (Turbine Erfurt)	21	FC Vorwärts Berlin	2	Motor Zwickau	0
1954–55	Turbine Erfurt		26	13	8	5	58.	25	34	Troger (Wismut Karl-Marx-Stadt)	22	Wismut Karl-Marx-Stadt	3	SC Empor Rostock	2
1956	Wismut Karl-Marx-Stadt		26	15	8	3	53.	21	38	Linder (Lokomotive Stendal)	18	Chemie Halle	2	FC Vorwärts Berlin	1
1957	Wismut Karl-Marx-Stadt		26	16	4	6	49.	28	36	Kaulmann (FC Vorwärts, Berlin)	15	1.FC Lokomotive Leipzig	2	SC Empor Rostock	1
1958	FC Vorwärts, Berlin		26	17	4	5	50.	24	38	Müller (FC Carl Zeiss Jena)	17	SC Einheit Dresden	2	1.FC Lokomotive Leipzig	1
1959	Wismut Karl-Marx-Stadt		26	17	5	4	44.	25	39	Bauchspiess (Chemie Zeitz)	18	BFC Dynamo Berlin	3	Wismut Karl-Marx-Stadt	2
1960	FC Vorwärts, Berlin		26	19	3	4	73.	28	41	Bauchspiess (Chemie Zeitz)	25	FC Carl Zeiss Jena	3	SC Empor Rostock	2
1961										No competition		BFC Dynamo Berlin	3	Wismut Karl-Marx-Stadt	2
1961–62	FC Vorwärts, Berlin		39	21	8	10	64.	49	50	Bialas (SC Empor Rostock)	23	Chemie Halle	3	BFC Dynamo Berlin	1
1962–63	FC Carl Zeiss Jena		26	17	5	4	49.	22	39	Ducke (P) (FC Carl Zeiss Jena)	20	Motor Zwickau	3	Chemie Zeitz	0
1963–64	Chemie Leipzig		26	13	9	4	38.	21	35	Backhauss (Lokomotive Stendal)	15	Aufbau Magdeburg	3	1.FC Lokomotive Leipzig	2
1964–65	FC Vorwärts, Berlin		26	17	3	6	51.	24	37	Bauchspiess (Chemie Leipzig)	14	Aufbau Magdeburg	2	Motor Jena	1
1965–66	FC Vorwärts, Berlin		26	15	4	7	44.	27	34	Frenzel (1.FC Lokomotive Leipzig)	22	Chemie Leipzig	1	Lokomotive Stendal	0
1966–67	FC Karl-Marx-Stadt		26	14	9	3	39.	23	37	Rentzsh Sachsenring Zwickau)	17	Motor Zwickau	3	Hansa Rostock	0
1967–68	FC Carl Zeiss Jena		26	17	5	4	51.	19	39	Kostmann (Hansa Rostock)	15	1.FC. Union Berlin	2	FC Carl Zeiss Jena	1
1968–69	FC Vorwärts, Berlin		26	15	4	7	47.	28	34	Kostmann (Hansa Rostock)	18	1.FC Magdeburg	4	Wismut Karl-Marx-Stadt	0
1969–70	FC Carl Zeiss Jena		26	16	7	3	50.	16	39	Skrowny (Chemie Leipzig)	12	FC Vorwärts, Berlin	4	1.FC Lokomitive Leipzig	2
1970–71	Dynamo Dresden		26	18	3	5	56.	29	39	Kreische (Dynamo Dresden)	17	Dynamo Dresden	2	BFC Dynamo Berlin	1
1971–72	1.FC Magdeburg		26	17	4	5	48.	23	38	Kreische (Dynamo Dresden)	14	FC Carl Zeiss Jena	2	Dynamo Dresden	1

Season	Champion club	P	W	D	L	F. A.	Pts	Leading League Goalscorer		FA Cup Final			
1972–73	Dynamo Dresden	26	18	6	2	61.30	42	Kreische (Dynamo Dresden)	26	1.FC Magdeburg	3	1.FC Lokomotive Leipzig	2
1973–74	1.FC Magdeburg	26	16	7	3	50.27	39	Matoul (1.FC Lokomotive Leipzig)	20	FC Carl Zeiss Jena	3	Dynamo Dresden	1
1974–75	1.FC Magdeburg	26	18	6	2	57.28	42	Vogel (Chemie Halle)	17	Sachsenring Zwickau*	2	Dynamo Dresden	2
1975–76	Dynamo Dresden	26	19	5	2	70.23	43	Kreische (Dynamo Dresden)	24	1.FC Lokomotive Leipzig	3	ASK Vorwärts Frankfurt	0
1976–77	Dynamo Dresden	26	16	6	4	66.27	38	Streich (1.FC Magdeburg)	17	Dynamo Dresden	3	1.FC Lokomotive Leipzig	2
1977–78	Dynamo Dresden	26	18	5	3	70.25	41	Havenstein (Chemie Böhlen)	15	1.FC Magdeburg	1	Dynamo Dresden	0
1978–79	BFC Dynamo Berlin	26	21	4	1	75.18	46	Streich (1.FC Magdeburg)	23	1.FC Magdeburg	1	BFC Dynamo Berlin	0
1979–80	BFC Dynamo Berlin	26	20	3	3	72.16	43	Kühn (1.FC Lokomotive Leipzig)	21	FC Carl Zeiss Jena	3	Rot Weiss Erfurt	1
1980–81	BFC Dynamo Berlin	26	17	5	4	74.31	39	Streich (1.FC Magdeburg)	19	1.FC Lokomotive Leipzig	4	ASK Vorwärts Frankfurt	1
1981–82	BFC Dynamo Berlin	26	18	5	3	74.27	41	Schnuphase (FC Carl Zeiss Jena)	19	Dynamo Dresden*	1	BFC Dynamo Berlin	1

MILLA (Cameroon)

GERMANY (WEST)

Season	Champion club				Leading League Goalscorer		FA Cup Final			
1945–46	Regional Leagues only						No competition			
1946–47										
1947–48	1.FC Nürnberg	2	1.FC Kaiserslautern	1	Schlienz (VfB Stuttgart)	31				
1948–49	VfB Mannheim	3	Borussia Dortmund	2	Preissler (Borussia Dortmund)	25				
1949–50	VfB Stuttgart	2	FC Kickers Offenbach	1	Vetter (VfL Osnabruch)	28				
1950–51	1.FC Kaiserlautern	2	Preussen Münster	1	Woitkowiak (Hamburg SV)	40				
1951–52	VfB Stuttgart	3	1.FC Saarbrucken	2	Siedl (Borussia Neuenkirchen)	27				
1952–53	1.FC Kaiserslautern	4	VfB Stuttgart	1	Walter (F) (1.FC Kaiserslautern)	38	Rot Weiss Essen	2	Alemannia Aachen	1
1953–54	Hanover 96	5	1.FC Kaiserslautern	1	Martin (1.FC Saarbrucken)	35	VfB Stuttgart	1	1.FC Köln	0
1954–55	Rot Weiss Essen	4	1.FC Kaiserslautern	3	Meyer (VfR Mannheim)	36	Karlsruher SC	3	Hamburg SV	1
1955–56	Borussia Dortmund	4	Karlsruher SC	2	Seeler (Hamburg SV)	32	Karsruher SC	3	Hamburg SV	1
1956–57	Borussia Dortmund	4	Hamburg SV	1	Beck (Karlsruher SC)	33	FC Bayern München	1	Fortuna Dusseldorf	0
1957–58	FC Schalke 04	3	Hamburg SV	0	Trapp (Tura Ludwigshafen)	29	VfB Stuttgart	4	Fortuna Dusseldorf	3
1958–59	Eintracht Frankfurt	5	FC Kickers Offenbach	3	Seeler (Hamburg SV)	29	Schwarz Weiss Essen	5	Borussia Neuenkirchen	2
1959–60	Hamburg SV	3	1.FC Köln	2	Seeler (Hamburg SV)	36	Borussia Mönchengladbach	3	Karlsruhe SC	2
1960–61	1.FC Nürnberg	3	Borussia Dortmund	0	Seeler (Hamburg SV)	30	Werder Bremen	2	1.FC Kaiserslautern	0
1961–62	1.FC Köln	4	1.FC Nürnberg	0	Dorrenbacher (Borussia Neuenkirchen)	37	1.FC Nürnberg	2	Fortuna Dusseldorf	1
1962–63	Borussia Dortmund	3	1.FC Köln	1	Altendorff (Hertha BSC, Berlin)	41	Hamburg SV	3	Borussia Dortmund	0
	Bundesliga Records		P W D L F. A. Pts							
1963–64	1.FC Köln		30 17 11 2 78.40 45		Seeler (Hamburg SV)	30	München 1860	2	Eintracht Frankfurt	0
1964–65	Werder Bremen		30 15 11 4 54.29 41		Brunnenmeier (München 1860)	24	Borussia Dortmund	2	Alemannia Aachen	0
1965–66	München 1860		34 20 10 4 80.40 50		Emmerich (Borussia Dortmund)	31	FC Bayern München	4	Meidericher SV	2
1966–67	Eintracht Braunschweig		34 17 9 8 49.27 43		Müller (G) FC Bayern München)	28	FC Bayern München	4	Hamburg SV	0
1967–68	1.FC Nürnberg		34 19 9 6 71.37 47		Löhr (1.FC Köln)	27	1.FC Köln	4	VfL Bochum	1
1968–69	FC Bayern München		34 18 10 6 61.31 46		Müller (G) (FC Bayern München)	30	FC Bayern München	2	FC Schalke 04	1
1969–70	Borussia Mönchengladbach		34 23 5 6 71.29 51		Müller (G) (FC Bayern München)	38	FC Kickers Offenbach	2	1.FC Köln	1
1970–71	Borussia Mönchengladbach		34 20 10 4 77.35 50		Kobluhn (Rot Weiss Oberhausen)	24	FC Bayern München	2	1.FC Köln	1
1971–72	FC Bayern München		34 24 7 3 101.38 55		Müller (G) (FC Bayern München)	40	FC Schalke 04	5	1.FC Kaiserslautern	0
1972–73	FC Bayern München		34 25 4 5 93.29 54		Müller (G) (FC Bayern München)	36	Borussia Mönchengladbach	2	1.FC Köln	1
1973–74	FC Bayern München		34 20 9 5 95.53 49		Heynckes (Borussia Mönchengladbach) Müller (G) (FC Bayern München)	30	Eintracht Frankfurt	3	Hamburg SV	1
1974–75	Borussia Mönchengladbach		34 21 8 5 86.40 50		Heynckes (Borussia Mönchengladbach)	27	Eintracht Frankfurt	1	MSV Duisburg	0

Season	Champion club	P	W	D	L	F. A.	Pts	Leading League Goalscorer		FA Cup Final			
1975–76	Borussia Mönchengladbach	34	16	13	5	66.37	45	Fischer (Schalke 04)	29	Hamburg SV	2	1.FC Kaiserslautern	0
1976–77	Borussia Mönchengladbach	34	17	10	7	58.34	44	Müller (D) (1.FC Köln)	34	1.FC Köln	2	Hertha BSC, Berlin	1
1977–78	1.FC Köln	34	22	4	8	86.41	48	Müller (G) (FC Bayern München) Müller (D) (1.FC Köln)	24	1.FC Köln	2	Fortuna Dusseldorf	0
1978–79	Hamburg SV	34	21	7	6	78.32	49	Allofs (K) (Fortuna Dusseldorf)	22	Fortuna Dusseldorf	1	Hertha BSC, Berlin	0
1979–80	FC Bayern München	34	22	6	6	84.33	50	Rummenigge (FC Bayern München)	26	Fortuna Dusseldorf	2	1.FC Köln	1
1980–81	FC Bayern München	34	22	9	3	89.41	53	Rummenigge (FC Bayern München)	29	Eintracht Frankfurt	3	1.FC Kaiserslautern	1
1981–82	Hamburg SV	34	18	12	4	95.45	48	Hrubesch (Hamburg SV)	27	FC Bayern München	4	1.FC Nürnberg	2

BELLOUMI (Algeria)

HOLLAND

Season	Champion club		FA Cup Final			
1945–46	Haarlem FC	Amateur, regional leagues only with national play-offs.	No competition			
1946–47	Ajax					
1947–48	B.V.V. (Den Bosch)		Wageningen*	0	D.W.V.	0
1948–49	S.V.V.		Quick*	1	Helmondia	1
1949–50	Limburgia		PSV Eindhoven	4	Haarlem	3
1950–51	P.S.V. Eindhoven		No competition			
1951–52	Willem II					
1952–53	R.C.H.					
1953–54	Eindhoven					
1954–55	Willem II					

Season	Professional champions	P	W	D	L	F.	A.	Pts.	Leading League Goalscorer		FA Cup Final			
1955–56	Sparta (Rotterdam)	34	18	10	6	60.	38	46	Lenstra (SC Enschede)	34				
1956–57	Ajax	34	22	5	7	64.	40	49	Dillen (PSV Eindhoven)	43	Fortuna '54	4	Feyenoord	2
1957–58	D.O.S. Utrecht	34	19	9	6	84.	52	47	Canjels (NAC Breda)	32	Sparta (Rotterdam)	4	Volendam	3
1958–59	Sparta (Rotterdam)	34	20	11	3	83.	30	51	Canjels (NAC Breda)	34	VV Venlo	4	ADO Den Haag	1
1959–60	Ajax	34	22	6	6	109.	44	50	Groot (H) (Ajax)	38	No competition			
1960–61	Feyenoord	34	24	5	5	100.	40	53	Groot (H) (Ajax)	41	Ajax	3	NAC Breda	0
1961–62	Feyenoord	34	20	10	4	88.	35	50	Tol (Volendam)	27	Sparta (Rotterdam)	1	DHC	0
1962–63	P.S.V. Eindhoven	30	17	8	5	67.	38	42	Kerkhoffs (PSV Eindhoven)	22	Willem II	3	ADO Den Haag	0
1963–64	DWS Amsterdam	30	19	5	6	58.	28	43	Geurtsen (DWS Amsterdam)	28	Fortuna '54*	0	ADO Den Haag	0
1964–65	Feyenoord	30	21	3	6	77.	30	45	Geurtsen (DWS Amsterdam)	23	Feyenoord	1	Go Ahead	0
1965–66	Ajax	30	24	4	2	79.	25	52	Kruiver (Feyenoord) Van der Kuijlen (PSV Eindhoven)	23	Sparta (Rotterdam)	1	ADO Den Haag	0
1966–67	Ajax	34	26	4	4	122.	34	56	Cruyff (Ajax)	33	Ajax	2	NAC Breda	1
1967–68	Ajax	34	27	4	3	96.	19	58	Kindvall (Feyenoord)	28	ADO Den Haag	2	Ajax	1
1968–69	Feyenoord	34	26	5	3	73.	21	57	Kindvall (Feyenoord) Van Dijk (FC Twente)	30	Feyenoord	3	PSV Eindhoven	1
1969–70	Ajax	34	27	6	1	100.	23	60	Van der Kuijlen (PSV Eindhoven)	26	Ajax	2	PSV Eindhoven	0
1970–71	Feyenoord	34	26	5	3	82.	24	57	Kindvall (Feyenoord)	24	Ajax	4	Sparta	3
1971–72	Ajax	34	30	3	1	104.	20	63	Cruyff (Ajax)	25	Ajax	3	FC Den Haag	2
1972–73	Ajax	34	30	0	4	104.	18	60	Brokamp (MVV Maastricht) Janssens (NEC Nijmegen)	18	NAC Breda	2	NEC Nijmegen	0
1973–74	Feyenoord	34	25	6	3	96.	28	56	Van der Kuijlen (PSV Eindhoven)	27	PSV Eindhoven	6	NAC Breda	0
1974–75	P.S.V. Eindhoven	34	23	9	2	82.	26	55	Geels (Ajax)	30	FC Den Haag	1	FC Twente	0
1975–76	P.S.V. Eindhoven	34	24	5	5	89.	27	53	Geels (Ajax)	29	PSV Eindhoven	1	Roda JC	0
1976–77	Ajax	34	23	6	5	62.	26	52	Geels (Ajax)	29	FC Twente	3	PEC Zwolle	0
1977–78	P.S.V. Eindhoven	34	21	11	2	74.	21	53	Geels (Ajax)	30	AZ'67 (Alkmaar)	1	Ajax	0
1978–79	Ajax	34	24	6	4	93.	31	54	Kist (AZ'67 Alkmaar)	34	Ajax	4	FC Twente	1
1979–80	Ajax	34	22	6	6	77.	41	50	Kist (AZ'67 Alkmaar)	25	Feyenoord	3	Ajax	1

Season	Champion club	P	W	D	L	F.	A.	Pts.	Leading League Goalscorer		FA Cup Final			
1980–81	AZ'67 Alkmaar	34	27	6	1	101	30	60	Geels (Sparta Rotterdam)	22	AZ'67 (Alkmaar)	3	Ajax	1
1981–82	Ajax	34	26	4	4	117	42	56	Kieft (Ajax)	32	AZ'67 (Alkmaar)	5	Utrecht	2

SANSOM (England)

HUNGARY

Season	Champion club	P	W	D	L	F. A.	Pts.	Leading League Goalscorer		FA Cup Final			
1945–46	Ujpest Dozsa	18	14	3	1	71.23	31	Deak (SZAC)	54				
1946–47	Ujpest Dozsa	30	21	5	4	106.43	47	Deak (SZAC)	48				
1947–48	Csepel, Budapest	32	24	4	4	73.32	52	Puskas (Kispest)	50				
1948–49	Ferencvaros	30	26	1	3	140.36	53	Deak (Ferencvaros)	59			No competition	
1949–50	Honved	30	23	4	3	84.29	50	Puskas (Honved)	31				
1950	Honved	15	13	1	1	67.16	27	Puskas (Honved)	25				
1951	MTK (Red Banner)	26	22	2	2	96.27	46	Kocsis (Honved)	30				
1952	Honved	26	21	5	0	88.21	47	Kocsis (Honved)	36	MTK (Red Banner)	3	Dorog	2
1953	MTK (Red Banner)	26	22	2	2	92.28	46	Puskas (Honved)	27			No competition	
1954	Honved	26	19	2	5	100.43	40	Kocsis (Honved)	33				
1955	Honved	26	20	5	1	99.47	45	Czibor (Honved)	20	Vasas Budapest	3	Honved	2
1956		Championship abandoned											
1957	Vasas Budapest	11	7	3	1	36.14	17	Szilagyi (Vasas Budapest)	17			No competition	
1957–58	MTK (Red Banner)	26	15	5	6	51.30	35	Friedmanszky (Ferencvaros)	16	Ferencvaros	2	Salgotarjan	1
1958–59	Csepel, Budapest	26	14	6	6	56.25	34	Tichy (Honved)	15				
1959–60	Ujpest Dozsa	26	17	6	3	52.26	40	Albert (Ferencvaros)	27				
1960–61	Vasas Budapest	26	15	8	3	59.24	38	Tichy (Honved) Albert (Ferencvaros)	21			No competition	
1961–62	Vasas Budapest	26	17	4	5	55.27	38	Tichy (Honved)	23				
1962–63	Ferencvaros	26	15	7	4	49.28	37	Bene (Ujpest Dozsa)	23				
1963	Vasas Gyor	13	6	5	2	20. 7	17	Tichy (Honved)	13				
1964	Ferencvaros	26	19	3	4	58.27	41	Tichy (Honved)	28	Honved	1	Vasas Gyor	0
1965	Vasas Budapest	26	17	5	4	48.19	39	Albert (Ferencvaros)	27	Vasas Gyor	4	Diosgyor	0
1966	Vasas Budapest	26	17	9	0	67.27	43	Farkas (Vasas Budapest)	25	Vasas Gyor	4	Ferencvaros	3
1967	Ferencvaros	30	24	4	2	85.24	52	Dunai (A) (Ujpest Dozsa)	36	Vasas Gyor	1	Salgotarjan	0
1968	Ferencvaros	30	21	7	2	65.26	49	Dunai (A) (Ujpest Dozsa)	31	MTK	2	Honved	1
1969	Ujpest Dozsa	30	20	8	2	83.27	48	Bene (Ujpest Dozsa)	27	Ujpest Dozsa	3	Honved	1
1970	Ujpest Dozsa	14	11	1	2	37.13	23	Dunai (A) (Ujpest Dozsa)	14	Ujpest Dozsa	3	Komlo	2
1970–71	Ujpest Dozsa	30	18	7	5	71.29	43	Kozma (Honved)	25			No competition	
1971–72	Ujpest Dozsa	30	20	6	4	78.30	46	Bene (Ujpest Dozsa)	29	Ferencvaros	2	Tatabanya	1
1972–73	Ujpest Dozsa	30	21	4	3	81.21	46	Bene (Ujpest Dozsa)	23	Vasas Budapest	4	Honved	3
1973–74	Ujpest Dozsa	30	18	6	6	75.33	42	Kozma (Honved)	27	Ferencvaros	3	Banyasz Komloi	1
1974–75	Ujpest Dozsa	28	20	5	3	71.33	45	Bene (Ujpest Dozsa) Kozma (Honved)	20	Ujpest Dozsa	3	Szombathely Haladas	2
1975–76	Ferencvaros	30	20	6	4	65.38	46	Fazekas (Ujpest Dozsa)	19	Ferencvaros	1	MTK-VM	0
1976–77	Vasas Budapest	34	25	3	6	100.45	53	Varadi (Vasas Budapest)	36	Diosgyor (Mini-League)			
1977–78	Ujpest Dozsa	34	19	13	2	95.46	51	Fazekas (Ujpest Dozsa)	24	Ferencvaros	4	Pecs MSC	2
1978–79	Ujpest Dozsa	34	21	10	3	84.38	52	Fekete (Ujpest Dozsa)	31	Raba ETO Gyor	1	Ferencvaros	0
1979–80	Honved	34	19	10	5	67.38	48	Fazekas (Ujpest Dozsa)	36	Diosgyor	3	Vasas Budapest	1
1980–81	Ferencvaros	34	21	9	4	75.33	51	Nyilasi (Ferencvaros)	30	Vasas Budapest	1	Diosgyor	0
1981–82	Raba ETO Gyor	34	21	7	6	102.50	49	Hannich (Raba ETO Gyor)	22	Ujpest Dozsa	2	Videoton	0

PLATINI (France)

IRELAND (NORTH)

Season	Champion club	P	W	D	L	F. A.	Pts.	Leading League Goalscorer		FA Cup Final			
1945–46	Linfield	20	17	0	3	79.27	34	Walsh (Linfield)	28	Linfield	3	Distillery	0
1946–47	Belfast Celtic	28	21	2	5	95.40	44	McMorran (Belfast Celtic)	30	Belfast Celtic	1	Glentoran	0
1947–48	Belfast Celtic	22	19	1	2	84.26	39	Jones (Belfast Celtic)	28	Linfield	3	Coleraine	0
1948–49	Linfield	22	16	4	2	58.21	36	Simpson (Linfield)	19	Derry City	3	Glentoran	1
1949–50	Linfield	22	17	4	1	64.27	38	Hughes (Glentoran)	23	Linfield	2	Distillery	1
1950–51	Glentoran	22	18	2	2	66.21	38	Allen (Portadown) Hughes (Glentoran)	23	Glentoran	3	Ballymena	1
1951–52	Glenavon	22	17	3	2	67.19	37	Jones (Glenavon)	27	Ards	1	Glentoran	0
1952–53	Glentoran	22	14	5	3	59.25	33	Hughes (Glentoran)	28	Linfield	5	Coleraine	0
1953–54	Linfield	22	15	6	1	56.26	36	Jones (Glenavon)	32	Derry City	3	Glentoran	2
1954–55	Linfield	22	15	6	1	46.21	36	Coyle (Coleraine)	20	Dundela	3	Glenavon	0
1955–56	Linfield	22	19	2	1	56.16	40	Jones (Glenavon)	26	Distillery	4	Glentoran	1
1956–57	Glenavon	22	16	3	3	71.22	35	Jones (Glenavon)	33	Glenavon	2	Derry City	0
1957–58	Ards	22	16	4	2	68.32	36	Milburn (Linfield)	29	Ballymena	2	Linfield	0
1958–59	Linfield	22	17	0	5	69.27	34	Milburn (Linfield)	26	Glenavon	2	Ballymena	0
1959–60	Glenavon	22	17	1	4	67.28	35	Jones (Glenavon)	29	Linfield	5	Ards	1
1960–61	Linfield	22	14	4	4	65.34	32	Thompson (Glentoran)	22	Glenavon	5	Linfield	1
1961–62	Linfield	22	14	3	5	62.32	31	Lynch (Ards)	20	Linfield	4	Portadown	0
1962–63	Distillery	22	13	5	4	57.30	31	Meldrum (Distillery)	27	Linfield	2	Distillery	1
1963–64	Glentoran	22	14	5	3	59.29	33	Thompson (Glentoran)	21	Derry City	2	Glentoran	0
1964–65	Derry City	22	15	5	2	62.32	35	Guy (Glenavon) Halliday (Coleraine)	19	Coleraine	2	Glenavon	1
1965–66	Linfield	22	14	6	2	68.23	34	Pavis (Linfield)	28	Glentoran	2	Linfield	0
1966–67	Glentoran	22	14	6	2	67.35	34	Pavis (Linfield)	25	Crusaders	3	Glentoran	1
1967–68	Glentoran	22	17	3	2	79.24	37	Pavis (Linfield)	30	Crusaders	2	Linfield	0
1968–69	Linfield	22	17	1	4	61.19	35	Hale (Derry City)	21	Ards	4	Distillery	2
1969–70	Glentoran	22	14	6	2	46.17	34	Dickson (Coleraine)	21	Linfield	2	Ballymena	1
1970–71	Linfield	22	18	2	2	58.16	38	Hamilton (Linfield)	18	Distillery	3	Derry City	0
1971–72	Glentoran	22	14	5	3	50.17	33	Dickson (Coleraine) Watson (Distillery)	15	Coleraine	2	Portadown	1
1972–73	Crusaders	22	14	4	4	50.22	32	Dickson (Coleraine)	23	Glentoran	3	Linfield	2
1973–74	Coleraine	22	16	3	3	41.20	35	Dickson (Coleraine)	24	Ards	2	Ballymena	1
1974–75	Linfield	22	17	3	2	53.23	37	Malone (Portadown)	19	Coleraine	2	Linfield	1
1975–76	Crusaders	22	15	6	1	51.19	36	Dickson (Coleraine)	23	Carrick Rangers	2	Linfield	1
1976–77	Glentoran	22	17	2	3	50.19	36	McAteer (Crusaders)	20	Coleraine	4	Linfield	1
1977–78	Linfield	22	19	2	1	65.22	40	Feeney (Glentoran)	17	Linfield	3	Ballymena	1
1978–79	Linfield	22	14	6	2	46.21	34	Armstrong (Ards)	21	Cliftonville	3	Portadown	2
1979–80	Linfield	22	19	1	2	59.17	39	Martin (Glentoran)	17	Linfield	2	Crusaders	0
1980–81	Glentoran	22	15	7	0	59.26	37	Dickson (Coleraine) Malone (Ballymena)	18	Ballymena	1	Glenavon	0
1981–82	Linfield	22	17	3	2	59.21	37	Blackledge (Glentoran)	18	Linfield	2	Coleraine	1

MARADONA (Argentina)

ITALY

Season	Champion club	P	W	D	L	F.	A.	Pts.	Leading League Goalscorer		FA Cup Final
1945–46	Torino	40	30	4	6	108.	32	64			
1946–47	Torino	38	28	7	3	104.	35	63	Mazzola (V) (Torino)	29	
1947–48	Torino	40	29	7	4	125.	33	65	Boniperti (Juventus)	27	
1948–49	Torino	38	25	10	3	78.	34	60	Nyers (Inter)	26	
1949–50	Juventus	38	28	6	4	100.	43	62	Nordahl (AC Milan)	35	
1950–51	AC Milan	38	26	8	4	107.	39	60	Nordahl (AC Milan)	34	
1951–52	Juventus	38	26	8	4	98.	34	60	Hansen (J) (Juventus)	30	No competition
1952–53	Internazionale (Milan)	34	19	9	6	46.	24	47	Nordahl (AC Milan)	26	
1953–54	Internazionale (Milan)	34	20	11	3	67.	32	51	Nordahl (AC Milan)	23	
1954–55	AC Milan	34	19	10	5	81.	35	48	Nordahl (AC Milan)	27	
1955–56	Fiorentina	34	20	13	1	59.	20	53	Pivatelli (Bologna)	29	
1956–57	AC Milan	34	21	6	7	65.	40	48	Da Costa (AS Roma)	22	
1957–58	Juventus	34	23	5	6	77.	44	51	Charles (Juventus)	28	Lazio (Rome)
1958–59	AC Milan	34	20	12	2	84.	32	52	Angelillo (Inter)	33	Juventus
1959–60	Juventus	34	25	5	4	92.	33	55	Sivori (Juventus)	27	Juventus
1960–61	Juventus	34	22	5	7	80.	42	49	Brighenti (Sampdoria)	27	Fiorentina
1961–62	AC Milan	34	24	5	5	83.	36	53	Milani (Fiorentina) Altafini (AC Milan)	22	Napoli
1962–63	Internazionale (Milan)	34	19	11	4	56.	20	49	Nielsen (Bologna) Manfredini (AS Roma)	19	Atlanta (Bergamo)
1963–64	Bologna	34	22	10	2	54.	18	54	Nielsen (Bologna)	21	AS Roma
1964–65	Internazionale (Milan)	34	22	10	2	68.	29	54	Mazzola (S) (Inter) Orlando (Fiorentina)	17	Juventus
1965–66	Internazionale (Milan)	34	20	10	4	70.	28	50	Vinicio (Lanerossi)	25	Fiorentina
1966–67	Juventus	34	18	13	3	44.	19	49	Riva (Cagliari)	18	AC Milan
1967–68	AC Milan	30	18	10	2	53.	24	46	Prati (AC Milan)	15	Torino
1968–69	Fiorentina	30	16	13	1	38.	18	45	Riva (Cagliari)	20	AS Roma
1969–70	Cagliari	30	17	11	2	42.	11	45	Riva (Cagliari)	21	Bologna
1970–71	Internazionale (Milan)	30	19	8	3	50.	26	46	Boninsegna (Inter)	24	Torino
1971–72	Juventus	30	17	9	4	48.	24	43	Boninsegna (Inter)	24	AC Milan
1972–73	Juventus	30	18	9	3	45.	22	45	Savoldi (Bologna) Rivera (AC Milan) Pulici (Torino)	17	AC Milan
1973–74	Lazio (Rome)	30	18	7	5	45.	23	43	Chinaglia (Lazio)	24	Bologna
1974–75	Juventus	30	18	7	5	49.	19	43	Pulici (Torino)	18	Fiorentina
1975–76	Torino	30	18	9	3	49.	22	45	Pulici (Torino)	21	Napoli
1976–77	Juventus	30	23	5	2	50.	20	51	Graziani (Torino)	21	AC Milan
1977–78	Juventus	30	15	14	1	46.	17	44	Rossi (Lanerossi)	24	Internazionale
1978–79	AC Milan	30	17	10	3	46.	19	44	Giordano (Lazio)	19	Juventus
1979–80	Internazionale (Milan)	30	14	13	3	44.	25	41	Bettega (Juventus)	16	AS Roma

World Cup Gallery

Season	Champion club	P	W	D	L	F. A.	Pts	Leading League Goalscorer		FA Cup Final
1980–81	Juventus	30	17	10	3	46.15	44	Pruzzo (AS Roma)	18	AS Roma
1981–82	Juventus	30	19	8	3	48.14	46	Pruzzo (AS Roma)	15	Internazionale (Milan)

KARL-HEINZ FORSTER (W. Germany)

MALTA

Season	Champion club	P	W	D	L	F. A.	Pts	Leading League Goalscorer		FA Cup Final			
1945–46	Valletta	12	8	3	1	30.13	19			Sliema Wanderers	2	Hamrun Liberty	1
1946–47	Hamrun Spartans	14	10	1	3	29.13	21			Floriana	3	Valletta	0
1947–48	Valletta	14	10	3	1	44.16	23			Sliema Wanderers	3	Hibernians	2
1948–49	Sliema Wanderers	14	11	0	3	33.15	22			Floriana	5	Sliema Wanderers	1
1949–50	Floriana	14	11	1	2	42. 8	23			Floriana	3	St. George's	1
1950–51	Floriana	14	10	3	1	37.17	23			Sliema Wanderers	5	Hibernians	0
1951–52	Floriana	14	12	1	1	48.11	25	Borg (L) (Floriana)	18	Sliema Wanderers	5	Hibernians	4
1952–53	Floriana	14	10	2	2	27.12	22	Pace (Valletta)	9	Floriana	1	Sliema Wanderers	0
1953–54	Sliema Wanderers	14	9	2	3	31.16	20			Floriana	5	Rabat	1
1954–55	Floriana	14	13	0	1	40.7	26			Floriana	1	Sliema Wanderers	0
1955–56	Sliema Wanderers	14	12	0	2	48.12	24	Nicholl (Sliema)	15	Sliema Wanderers	1	Floriana	0
1956–57	Sliema Wanderers	14	12	2	0	43.6	26	Nicholl (Sliema)	14	Floriana	2	Valletta	0
1957–58	Floriana	14	12	0	2	43.7	24	D'Emanuele (Floriana)	14	Floriana	2	Sliema Wanderers	0
1958–59	Valletta	14	10	3	1	39.11	23	Urpani (Valletta) Zammit (Valletta) Azzopardi (Valletta)	8	Sliema Wanderers	2	Valletta	1
1959–60	Valletta	14	11	2	1	41. 8	24	Zammitt (Valletta)	13	Valletta	3	Floriana	0
1960–61	Hibernians	14	12	1	1	34.14	25	Cauchi (Floriana)	12	Floriana	2	Hibernians	0
1961–62	Floriana	14	14	0	0	43.10	28	Dalli (Floriana)	16	Hibernians	1	Valletta	0
1962–63	Valletta	14	11	2	1	46. 9	24	Azzopardi (Valletta)	20	Sliema Wanderers	2	Hibernians	0
1963–64	Sliema Wanderers	14	13	0	1	39.9	26	Borg (J) (Valletta)	11	Valletta	1	Sliema Wanderers	0
1964–65	Sliema Wanderers	12	9	2	1	36. 9	20	Cini (J) (Sliema)	12	Sliema Wanderers	4	Floriana	2
1965–66	Sliema Wanderers	10	8	2	0	24. 7	18	Bonett (Sliema) Cocks (Sliema)	6	Floriana	2	Hibernians	1
1966–67	Hibernians	10	6	4	0	15. 2	16	Delia (Hibernians)	8	Floriana	1	Hibernians	0
1967–68	Floriana	10	8	2	0	19. 2	18	Cini (J) (Sliema)	10	Sliema Wanderers	3	Hibernians	2
1968–69	Hibernians	14	9	3	2	28.15	21	Cassar (Hibernians)	9	Sliema Wanderers	3	Hamrun Spartans	2
1969–70	Floriana	14	9	4	1	19. 7	22			Hibernians	2	Valletta	1
1970–71	Sliema Wanderers	14	7	6	1	17. 5	20	Xuereb (R) (Floriana)	5	Hibernians	3	Sliema Wanderers	1
1971–72	Sliema Wanderers	19	11	6	2	19. 7	28	Giglio (Valletta)	9	Floriana	3	Sliema Wanderers	1
1972–73	Floriana	18	12	2	4	31.10	26	Borg (C) (Hamrun Spartans)	10	Gzira Utd	2	Birkirkara	0
1973–74	Valletta	18	12	4	2	23. 8	28	Camilleri (Sliema)	9	Sliema Wanderers	1	Floriana	0
1974–75	Floriana	18	14	3	1	36. 9	31	Xuereb (R) (Floriana)	17	Valletta	2	Hibernians	0
1975–76	Sliema Wanderers	18	11	4	3	35.13	26	Aquilina (Sliema)	9	Floriana	2	Valletta	0
1976–77	Floriana	18	15	3	0	53.12	33	Xuereb (Floriana)	16	Valletta	1	Floriana	0
1977–78	Valletta	18	12	4	2	44. 6	28	Farrugia (Valletta)	16	Valletta	3	Floriana	2
1978–79	Hibernians	6	5	1		12. 5	11	Brincat (Marsa) D'Emanuele (Hamrun Spartans)	9	Sliema Wanderers	2	Floriana	1
1979–80	Valletta	18	14	3	1	59. 8	31	Farrugia (Valletta) Cristiano (Valletta)	15	Hibernians	2	Sliema Wanderers	1

Season	Champion club	P	W	D	L	F.	A.	Pts	Leading League Goalscorer		FA Cup Final			
1980–81	Hibernians	14	12	2	0	34	10	26	Spiteri Gonzi (Hibernians)	13	Floriana	2	Senglea Athletic	1
1981–82	Hibernians	14	12	2	0	36	7	26	Spiteri Gonzi (Hibernians)	12	Hibernians	2	Sliema Wanderers	0

BERNARDES (Honduras)

POLAND

Season	Champion club	P	W	D	L	F. A.	Pts.	Leading League Goalscorer		FA Cup Final			
1946		No competition								No competition			
1947													
1948	Cracovia	26	17	4	5	61.26	38	Kohut (Wisla Krakow)	33				
1949	Wisla Krakow	22	13	4	5	50.21	30	Aniola (Lech Poznan)	20				
1950	Wisla Krakow	22	16	1	5	51.17	33	Aniola (Lech Poznan)	20				
1951	Wisla Krakow	22	13	6	3	43.13	32	Aniola (Lech Poznan)	20	Ruch Chorzow	2	Wisla Krakow	0
1952	Ruch Chorzow	Two groups & play-off						Cieslik (Ruch Chorzow)	11	Polonia Warsaw	1	Legia Warsaw	0
1953	Ruch Chorzow	22	17	4	1	51.14	38	Cieslik (Ruch Chorzow)	22			No competition	
1954	Polonia Bytom	20	9	6	5	36.22	24	Kempny (Polonia Bytom)	13	Gwardia Warsaw	3	Wisla Krakow	1
								Pohl (Legia Warsaw)					
1955	Legia Warsaw	22	12	4	6	48.21	28	Hachorek (Gwardia Warsaw)	16	Legia Warsaw	5	Lechia Gdansk	0
1956	Legia Warsaw	22	15	4	3	65.17	34	Kempny (Legia Warsaw)	21	Legia Warsaw	3	Gornik Zabrze	0
1957	Gornik Zabrze	22	15	3	4	58.24	33	Brychczy (Legia Warsaw)	19	LKS Lodz	2	Gornik Zabrze	1
1958	LKS Lodz	22	13	6	3	61.24	32	Soporek (LKS Lodz)	19	No Competition			
1959	Gornik Zabrze	22	16	4	2	55.23	36	Pohl (Gornik Zabrze)	21				
								Liberda (Polonia Bytom)					
1960	Ruch Chorzow	22	12	6	4	41.29	30	Norkowski (Polonia Bydgoszcz)	17				
1961	Gornik Zabrze	26	19	5	2	73.18	43	Pohl (Gornik Zabrze)	24				
1962	Polonia Bytom	Two groups & play-off						Liberda (Polonia Bytom)	16	Zaglebie Sosnowiec	2	Gornik Zabrze	1
1962–63	Gornik Zabrze	26	19	4	3	69.26	42	Kielec (Pogon Szczecin)	18	Zaglebie Sosnowiec	2	Ruch Chorzow	0
1963–64	Gornik Zabrze	26	17	6	3	59.24	40	Brychczy (Legia Warsaw)	18	Legia Warsaw	2	Polonia Bytom	1
								Galeczka (Zaglebie Sosnowiec)					
								Wilim (Szombierki Bytom)					
1964-65	Gornik Zabrze	26	15	7	4	61.35	37	Brychczy (Legia Warsaw)	20	Gornik Zabrze	4	Czarni Zagan	0
1965–66	Gornik Zabrze	26	19	4	3	62.24	42	Lubanski (Gornik Zabrze)	23	Legia Warsaw	2	Gornik Zabrze	1
1966–67	Gornik Zabrze	26	16	5	5	44.20	37	Lubanksi (Gornik Zabrze)	18	Wisla Krakow	2	Rakow Czestochowa	0
1967–68	Ruch Chorzow	26	14	10	2	56.26	38	Lubanski (Gornik Zabrze)	24	Gornik Zabrze	3	Ruch Chorzow	0
1968–69	Legia Warsaw	26	16	7	3	51.16	39	Lubanski (Gornik Zabrze)	22	Gornik Zabrze	2	Legia Warsaw	0
1969–70	Legia Warsaw	26	17	6	3	43.17	40	Jarosik (Zaglebie Sosnowiec)	18	Gornik Zabrze	3	Ruch Chorzow	1
1970–71	Gornik Zabrze	26	17	5	4	43.21	39	Jarosik (Zaglebie Sosnowiec)	13	Gornik Zabrze	3	Zaglebie Sosnowiec	1
1971–72	Gornik Zabrze	26	14	9	3	45.23	37	Szymczak (Gwardia Warsaw)	16	Gornik Zabrze	5	Legia Warsaw	2
1972–73	Stal Mielec	26	13	10	3	47.21	36	Lato (Stal Mielec)	13	Legia Warsaw*	0	Polonia Bytom	0
1973–74	Ruch Chorzow	30	14	13	3	53.23	41	Kapka (Wisla Krakow)	15	Ruch Chorzow	2	Gwardia Warsaw	0
1974–75	Ruch Chorzow	30	20	4	6	61.27	44	Lato (Stal Mielec)	19	Stal Rzeszow*	0	ROW Rybnik	0
1975–76	Stal Mielec	30	13	12	5	45.23	38	Kmiecik (Wisla Krakow)	20	Slask Wroclaw	2	Stal Mielec	0
1976–77	Slask Wroclaw	30	17	7	6	38.32	41	Mazur (Zaglebie Sosnowiec)	17	Zaglebie Sosnowiec	1	Polonia Bytom	0
1977–78	Wisla Krakow	30	13	13	4	35.23	39	Kmiecik (Wisla Krakow)	15	Zaglebie Sosnowiec	2	Piast Gliwice	0
1978–79	Ruch Chorzow	30	16	7	7	44.27	39	Kmiecik (Wisla Krakow)	17	Arka Gdynia	2	Wisla Krakow	1
1979–80	Szombierki Bytom	30	16	7	7	42.26	39	Kmiecik (Wisla Krakow)	24	Legia Warsaw	5	Lech Poznan	0
1980–81	Widzew Lodz	30	14	11	5	39.25	39	Adamczyk (Legia Warsaw)	18	Legia Warsaw	1	Pogon Szczecin	0
1981–82	Widzew Lodz	30	14	11	5	45.31	39	Kapica (Szombierki Bytom)	15	Lech Poznan	1	Pogon Szczecin	0

ANTOGNONI (Italy)

PORTUGAL

Season	Champion club	P	W	D	L	F. A.	Pts	Leading League Goalscorer		FA Cup Final			
1945–46	Belenenses	22	18	2	2	74.24	38	Peyroteo (Sporting Lisbon)	30	Sporting Lisbon	4	Atletico Lisboa	2
1946–47	Sporting Lisbon	26	23	1	2	123.40	47	Peyroteo (Sporting Lisbon)	43		No competition		
1947–48	Sporting Lisbon	26	20	1	5	92.40	41	Araujo (FC Porto)	36	Sporting Lisbon	3	Belenenses	1
1948–49	Sporting Lisbon	26	20	2	4	100.35	42	Peyroteo (Sporting Lisbon)	40	Benfica	2	Atletico Lisboa	1
1949–50	Benfica	26	21	3	2	86.33	45	Julio (Benfica)	27		No competition		
1950–51	Sporting Lisbon	26	21	3	2	91.28	45	Vasques (Sporting Lisbon)	29	Benfica	5	Academica Coimbra	1
1951–52	Sporting Lisbon	26	19	3	4	91.32	41	Aguas (Benfica)	28	Benfica	5	Sporting Lisbon	4
1952–53	Sporting Lisbon	26	19	5	2	77.22	43	Matateu (Belenenses)	29	Benfica	5	FC Porto	0
1953–54	Sporting Lisbon	26	20	3	3	80.25	43	Martins (Sporting Lisbon)	31	Sporting Lisbon	3	Vitoria Setubal	2
1954–55	Benfica	26	18	3	5	61.20	39	Matateu (Belenenses)	32	Benfica	2	Sporting Lisbon	1
1955–56	FC Porto	26	18	7	1	77.20	43	Aguas (Benfica)	28	FC Porto	2	Torriense	0
1956–57	Benfica	26	17	7	2	76.25	41	Aguas (Benfica)	30	Benfica	3	Sporting Covilha	1
1957–58	Sporting Lisbon	26	19	5	2	79.21	43	Arsenio (C.U.F.)	23	FC Porto	1	Benfica	0
1958–59	FC Porto	26	17	7	2	81.22	41	Aguas (Benfica)	26	Benfica	1	FC Porto	0
1959–60	Benfica	26	20	5	1	75.27	45	Edmur (Vitoria Guimaraes)	25	Belenenses	2	Sporting Lisbon	1
1960–61	Benfica	26	22	2	2	92.21	46	Aguas (Benfica)	27	Leixoes	2	FC Porto	0
1961–62	Sporting Lisbon	26	19	5	2	66.17	43	Azumir (FC Porto)	23	Benfica	3	Vitoria Setubal	0
1962–63	Benfica	26	23	2	1	81.25	48	Torres (Benfica)	26	Sporting Lisbon	1	Vitoria Guimaraes	0
1963–64	Benfica	26	21	4	1	103.26	46	Eusebio (Benfica)	28	Benfica	6	FC Porto	2
1964–65	Benfica	26	19	5	2	88.21	43	Eusebio (Benfica)	28	Vitoria Setubal	3	Benfica	1
1965–66	Sporting Lisbon	26	18	6	2	70.21	42	Eusebio (Benfica) Figueredo (Sporting Lisbon)	25	Sporting Braga	1	Vitoria Setubal	0
1966–67	Benfica	26	20	3	3	64.18	43	Eusebio (Benfica)	31	Vitoria Setubal	3	Academica Coimbra	2
1967–68	Benfica	26	18	5	3	75.19	41	Eusebio (Benfica)	42	FC Porto	2	Vitoria Setubal	1
1968–69	Benfica	26	16	7	3	49.17	39	Antonio (Academica Coimbra)	19	Benfica	2	Academica Coimbra	1
1969–70	Sporting Lisbon	26	21	4	1	61.17	46	Eusebio (Benfica)	20	Benfica	3	Sporting Lisbon	1
1970–71	Benfica	26	18	5	3	62.17	41	Jorge (Benfica)	22	Sporting Lisbon	4	Benfica	1
1971–72	Benfica	30	26	3	1	81.16	55	Jorge (Benfica)	27	Benfica	3	Sporting Lisbon	2
1972–73	Benfica	30	28	2	0	101.15	58	Eusebio (Benfica)	40	Sporting Lisbon	3	Vitoria Setubal	2
1973–74	Sporting Lisbon	30	23	3	4	96.21	49	Yazalde (Sporting Lisbon)	46	Sporting Lisbon	2	Benfica	1
1974–75	Benfica	30	21	7	2	62.12	49	Yazalde (Sporting Lisbon)	30	Boavista	2	Benfica	1
1975–76	Benfica	30	23	4	3	94.20	50	Jordao (Benfica)	30	Boavista	2	Vitoria Guimaraes	1
1976–77	Benfica	30	23	5	2	67.24	51	Gomes da Silva (FC Porto)	26	FC Porto	1	Sporting Braga	0
1977–78	FC Porto	30	22	7	1	81.21	51	Gomes da Silva (FC Porto)	24	Sporting Lisbon	3	FC Porto	2
1978–79	FC Porto	30	21	8	1	70.19	50	Gomes da Silva (FC Porto)	27	Boavista	2	Sporting Lisbon	1
1979–80	Sporting Lisbon	30	24	4	2	67.17	52	Nene (Benfica) Jordao (Sporting Lisbon)	30	Benfica	1	FC Porto	0
1980–81	Benfica	30	22	6	2	72.14	50	Nene (Benfica)	20	Benfica	3	FC Porto	1
1981–82	Sporting Lisbon	30	19	8	3	66.26	46	Jacques (FC Porto)	27	Sporting Lisbon	4	Sporting Braga	0

VANDENBERGH (Belgium)

ROMANIA

Season	Champion club	P	W	D	L	F. A.	Pts.	Leading League Goalscorer		FA Cup Final			
1945–46		No competition								No competition			
1946–47	I.T. Arad	26	20	4	2	94.35	44	Bonyhadi (I.T. Arad)	26				
1947–48	I.T. Arad	30	22	6	2	129.31	50	Bonyhadi (I.T. Arad)	49	I.T. Arad	3	C.F.R. Timisoara	2
1948–49	I.C. Oradea	26	16	5	5	60.36	37	Vaczi (I.C. Oradea)	21	C.C.A. Bucharest	2	C.S.U. Cluj	1
1950	Flamura Rosie (U.T. Arad)	22	11	6	5	43.27	28	Radulescu (Rapid Bucharest)	18	C.C.A. Bucharest	3	Flamura Rosie (U.T. Arad)	1
1951	C.C.A. Bucharest	22	13	6	3	43.19	32	Vaczi (I.C. Oradea)	22	C.C.A. Bucharest	3	Flacara Medias	1
1952	C.C.A. Bucharest	22	15	6	1	46.16	36	Ozon (Dinamo Bucharest)	17	C.C.A. Bucharest	2	Flacara Ploesti	0
1953	C.C.A. Bucharest	21	11	6	4	27.14	28	Ozon (Dinamo Bucharest)	13	Flamura Rosie	1	C.C.A. Bucharest (U.T. Arad)	0
1954	Flamura Rosie (U.T. Arad)	26	15	5	6	37.29	35	Ene (Dinamo Bucharest)	20	Metalul Resita	2	Dinamo Bucharest	0
1955	Dinamo Bucharest	24	15	7	2	42.19	37	Ciosescu (Stiinta Timisoara)	18	C.C.A. Bucharest	6	Progresul Oradea	3
1956	C.C.A. Bucharest	24	15	3	6	64.28	33	Alexandrescu (C.C.A. Bucharest)	18	Progresul Oradea	2	Metalul C. Turzii	0
1957–58	Petrolul Ploesti	22	12	3	7	36.22	27	Ciosescu (Stiinta Timisoara)	21	Stiinta Timisoara	1	Progresul Bucharest	0
1958–59	Petrolul Ploesti	22	15	1	6	47.23	31	Ene (Rapid Bucharest)	18	Dinamo Bucharest	4	C.S.M. Baia Mare	0
1959–60	C.C.A. Bucharest	22	15	4	3	52.25	34	Constantin (C.C.A. Bucharest)	20	Progresul Bucharest	2	Dinamo Obor	0
1960–61	C.C.A. Bucharest	26	17	3	6	61.36	37	Constantin (C.C.A. Bucharest)	22	Ariesul Turda	2	Rapid Bucharest	1
1961–62	Dinamo Bucharest	26	14	8	4	62.35	36	Constantin (Steaua Bucharest)	24	Steaua Bucharest	5	Rapid Bucharest	1
1962–63	Dinamo Bucharest	27	14	9	4	46.25	37	Ionescu (Rapid Bucharest)	20	Petrolul Ploesti	6	Siderurgistul Galati	1
1963–64	Dinamo Bucharest	26	18	4	4	65.25	40	Fratila (Dinamo Bucharest) Pavlovic (Steaua Bucharest)	19	Dinamo Bucharest	5	Steaua Bucharest	3
1964–65	Dinamo Bucharest	26	17	4	5	56.22	38	Adam (Universitatea Cluj)	18	Stiinta Cluj	2	Dinamo Pitești	1
1965–66	Petrolul Ploesti	26	16	6	4	47.24	38	Ionescu (Rapid Bucharest)	24	Steaua Bucharest	4	Foresta Falticeni	0
1966–67	Rapid Bucharest	26	13	8	5	39.21	34	Oblemenco (Universitatea Craiova)	17	Steaua Bucharest	6	Foresta Falticeni	0
1967–68	Steaua Bucharest	26	14	7	5	45.26	35	Adam (Universitatea Cluj)	15	Dinamo Bucharest	3	Rapid Bucharest	1
1968–69	U.T. Arad	30	17	4	9	50.27	38	Dumitrache (Dinamo Bucharest)	22	Steaua Bucharest	2	Dinamo Bucharest	1
1969–70	U.T. Arad	30	18	3	9	54.42	39	Oblemenco (Universitatea Craiova)	19	Steaua Bucharest	2	Dinamo Bucharest	1
1970–71	Dinamo Bucharest	30	13	10	7	49.31	36	Tataru (Steaua Bucharest) Dumitrache (Dinamo Bucharest) Moldoveanu (Politehnica Jasi)	15	Steaua Bucharest	3	Dinamo Bucharest	2
1971–72	FC Arges Pitesti	30	19	3	8	51.35	41	Oblemenco (Universitatea Craiova)	20	Rupid Bucharest	2	Jiul Petroseni	0
1972–73	Dinamo Bucharest	30	17	5	8	51.32	39	Oblemenco (Universitatea Craiova)	21	Chimia Ramnicu Vilcea	4	Constructorul Galati	1
1973–74	Universitatea Craiova	34	20	5	9	63.37	45	Adam (Caile Ferate Romine)	23	Jiul Petroseni	4	Politehnica Timisoara	2
1974–75	Dinamo Bucharest	34	19	5	10	63.37	43	Georgescu (Dinamo Bucharest)	33	Rapid Bucharest	2	Universitatea Craiova	1
1975–76	Steaua Bucharest	34	21	9	4	79.33	51	Georgescu (Dinamo Bucharest)	31	Steaua Bucharest	1	CSU Galati	0
1976–77	Dinamo Bucharest	34	20	9	5	84.34	49	Georgescu (Dinamo Bucharest)	47	Universitatea Craiova	2	Steaua Bucharest	1
1977–78	Steaua Bucharest	34	17	7	10	75.49	41	Georgescu (Dinamo Bucharest)	24	Universitatea Craiova	3	Olimpia Satu Mare	1
1978–79	FC Arges Pitesti	34	20	5	9	54.29	45	Radu II (FC Arges Pitesti)	22	Steaua Bucharest	3	Sp. Studentzesc Bucharest	0

Season	Champion club	P	W	D	L	F.	A.	Pts.	Leading League Goalscorer		FA Cup Final			
1979–80	Universitatea Craiova	34	17	10	7	66	31	44	Cimpeanu II (Cluj-Napoka)	24	Politehnica Timisoara	2	Steaua Bucharest	1
1980–81	Universitatea Craiova	34	21	4	9	72	33	46	Radu II (FC Arges Pitesti)	28	Universitatea Craiova	6	Politehnica Timisoara	0
1981–82	Dinamo Bucharest	34	20	7	7	62	31	47	Iordanescu (Steaua Bucharest)	20	Dinamo Bucharest	3	FC Baia Mare	2

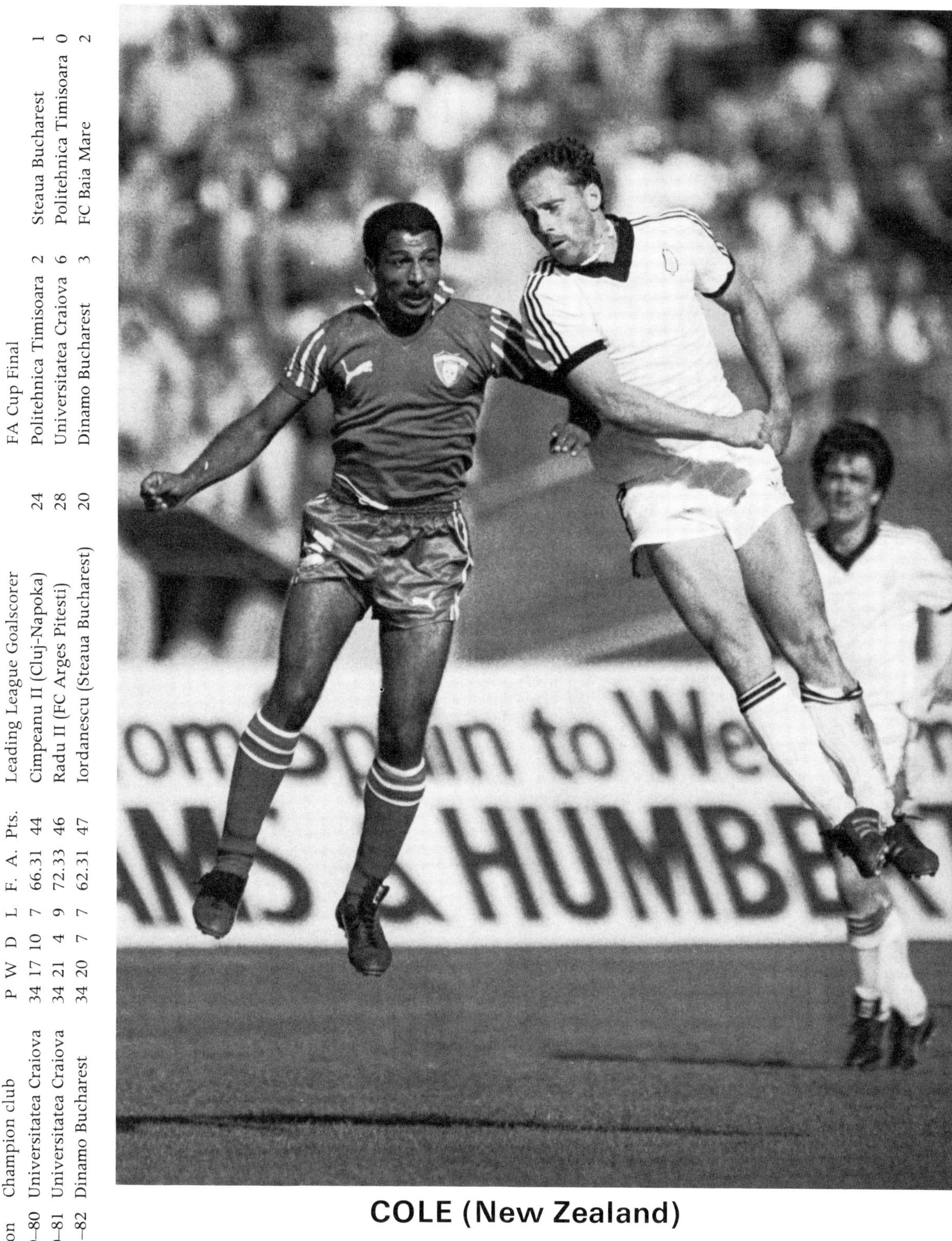

COLE (New Zealand)

RUSSIA

Season	Champion club	P	W	D	L	F. A.	Pts.	Leading League Goalscorer		FA Cup Final			
1945	Dynamo Moscow	22	19	2	1	73.13	40	Bobrov (ZDSA Moscow)	24	ZDSA Moscow	2	Dynamo Moscow	1
1946	ZDSA Moscow	22	17	3	2	55.13	37	Ponomarev (Torpedo Moscow)	18	Spartak Moscow	3	Dynamo Tbilissi	2
1947	ZDSA Moscow	24	17	6	1	61.16	40	Bobrov (ZDSA Moscow) Nikolaev (ZDSA Moscow)	14	Spartak Moscow	2	Torpedo Moscow	0
1948	ZDSA Moscow	26	19	3	4	82.30	41	Solovev (Dynamo Moscow)	25	ZDSA Moscow	3	Spartak Moscow	0
1949	Dynamo Moscow	34	26	5	3	104.30	57	Simonian (Spartak Moscow)	26	Torpedo Moscow	2	Dynamo Moscow	1
1950	ZDSA Moscow	36	20	13	3	91.31	53	Simonian (Spartak Moscow)	34	Sparktak Moscow	3	Dynamo Moscow	0
1951	ZDSA Moscow	28	18	7	3	53.19	43	Gogoberidze (Dynamo Tbilissi)	16	ZDSA Moscow	2	Kalinin	0
1952	Spartak Moscow	13	9	2	2	26.12	20	Zazroev (Dynamo Kiev)	11	Torpedo Moscow	1	Spartak Moscow	0
1953	Spartak Moscow	20	11	7	2	47.15	29	Simonian (Spartak Moscow) Gogoberidze (Dyamo Tbilissi)	14	Dynamo Moscow	1	Kryla Soviet (Kuybishev)	0
1954	Dynamo Moscow	24	15	5	4	44.20	35	Ilin (A) (Spartak Moscow Ilin (V) (Dynamo Moscow) Sochnev (Tr.R.Leningrad)	11	Dynamo Kiev	2	Spartak Erevan	1
1955	Dynamo Moscow	22	15	4	3	52.16	34	Parshin (Spartak Moscow)	13	ZDSA Moscow	2	Dynamo Moscow	1
1956	Spartak Moscow	22	15	4	3	68.28	34	Buzunov (ODO Sverdlovsk)	17	No Competition			
1957	Dynamo Moscow	22	16	4	2	49.15	36	Buzunov (ZDSA Moscow)	16	Lokomotiv Moscow	1	Spartak Moscow	0
1958	Spartak Moscow	22	13	6	3	55.28	32	Ilin (A) (Spartak Moscow)	19	Spartak Moscow	1	Torpedo Moscow	0
1959	Dynamo Moscow	22	13	5	4	42.21	31	Kaloev (Dynamo Tbilissi)	16	No Competition			
1960	Torpedo Moscow	30	29	5	5	56.25	45	Kaloev (Dynamo Tbilissi)	20	Torpedo Moscow	4	Dynamo Tbilissi	3
1961	Dynamo Kiev	30	18	9	3	58.28	45	Gusarov (Torpedo Moscow)	22	Shaktor Donezk	3	Torpedo Moscow	1
1962	Spartak Moscow	22	14	4	4	37.18	32	Sevidov (Spartak Moscow) Markarov (Neftchi Baku)	16	Shaktor Donezk	2	Znamia Truda (Orehovo-Zuevo)	0
1963	Dynamo Moscow	38	21	13	4	47.14	55	Kopaev (ASK Rostov)	27	Spartak Moscow	2	Shaktor Donezk	1
1964	Dynamo Tbilissi	32	18	10	4	48.30	46	Fedotov (ZDSA Moscow)	16	Dynamo Kiev	1	Kryla Soviet (Kuybishev)	0
1965	Torpedo Moscow	32	22	7	3	55.21	51	Kopaev (ASK Rostov)	18	Spartak Moscow	2	Dynamo Minsk	1
1966	Dynamo Kiev	36	23	10	3	66.17	56	Datunashivili (Dynamo Tbilissi)	20	Dynamo Kiev	2	Torpedo Moscow	0
1967	Dynamo Kiev	36	21	12	3	51.11	54	Mustigin (Dynamo Minsk)	19	Dynamo Kiev	3	ZDSA Moscow	0
1968	Dynamo Kiev	38	21	15	2	58.25	57	Abduraimov (Paktakor Tashkent) Gavasheli (Dynamo Tbilissi) Proskurin (ASK Rostove) Herhadze (Torpedo Kutaisi)	22	Torpedo Moscow	1	Paktakor Tashkent	0
1969	Spartak Moscow	26	19	5	2	40.11	43	Osianin (Spartak Moscow)	16	Karpaty Lvov	2	ASK Rostov	1
1970	ZDSA Moscow	32	20	5	7	46.17	45	Nodia (Dynamo Tbilissi)	17	Dynamo Moscow	2	Dynamo Tbilissi	1
1971	Dynamo Kiev	30	17	10	3	41.17	44	Malofeev (Dynamo Minsk)	16	Spartak Moscow	3	ASK Rostov	2
1972	Zarja Voroshilovgrad	30	15	10	5	52.30	40	Blokhin (Dynamo Kiev)	14	Torpedo Moscow*	1	Spartak Moscow	1
1973	Ararat Erevan	30	18	7	5	52.26	39	Blokhin (Dynamo Kiev)	18	Ararat Erevan	2	Dynamo Kiev	1
1974	Dynamo Kiev	30	14	12	4	49.24	40	Blokhin (Dynamo Kiev)	20	Dynamo Kiev	3	Zarja Voroshilovgrad	0
1975	Dynamo Kiev	30	17	9	4	53.30	43	Blokhin (Dynamo Kiev)	18	Ararat Erevan	2	Zarja Voroshilovgrad	1

World Cup Gallery

Season	Champion club	P	W	D	L	F.	A	Pts	Leading League Goalscorer		FA Cup Final			
1976	Dynamo Moscow (Spring)	15	9	4	2	17.	8	22	Andreasian (Ararat Erevan)	8	Dynamo Tbilissi	3	Ararat Erevan	0
	Torpedo Moscow (Autumn)	15	9	2	4	20.	9	20	Markin (Zenith Leningrad)	13				
1977	Dynamo Kiev	30	14	15	1	51.	12	43	Blokhin (Dynamo Kiev)	17	Dynamo Moscow	1	Torpedo Moscow	0
1978	Dynamo Tbilissi	30	17	8	5	45.	24	42	Yartsev (Spartak Moscow)	19	Dynamo Kiev	2	Shaktor Donezk	1
1979	Spartak Moscow*	34	21	10	3	66.	25	50	Staruchin (Shaktor Donezk)	26	Dynamo Moscow*	0	Dynamo Tbilissi	0
1980	Dynamo Kiev	34	21	9	4	63.	23	51	Andreev (ASK Rostov)	20	Shaktor Donezk	2	Dynamo Tbilissi	1
1981	Dynamo Kiev	34	22	9	3	58.	26	53	Shengelia (Dynamo Tbilissi)	23	ASK Rostov	1	Spartak Moscow	0
1982											Dynamo Kiev	1	Torpedo Moscow	0

DAHLEB (Algeria)

SCOTLAND

Season	Champion club	P	W	D	L	F. A.	Pts.	Leading League Goalscorer		FA Cup Final			
1945–46		No competition								No competition			
1946–47	Rangers	30	21	4	5	76.26	46	Mitchell (Third Lanark)	22	Aberdeen	2	Hibernian	1
1947–48	Hibernian	30	22	4	4	86.27	48	Aikman (Falkirk)	20	Rangers	2	Morton	1
1948–49	Rangers	30	20	6	4	63.32	46	Stoss (Dundee)	30	Rangers	4	Clyde	1
1949–50	Rangers	30	22	6	2	58.26	50	Bauld (Hearts)	30	Rangers	3	East Fife	0
1950–51	Hibernian	30	22	4	4	78.26	48	Reilly (Hibernian)	22	Celtic	1	Motherwell	0
1951–52	Hibernian	30	20	5	5	92.36	45	Reilly (Hibernian)	27	Motherwell	4	Dundee	0
1952–53	Rangers	30	18	7	5	80.39	43	Reilly (Hibernian) Fleming (East Fife)	30	Rangers	2	Aberdeen	1
1953–54	Celtic	30	20	3	7	72.29	43	Wardhaugh (Herts)	27	Celtic	2	Aberdeen	1
1954–55	Aberdeen	30	24	1	5	73.26	49	Bauld (Hearts)	21	Clyde	2	Celtic	1
1955–56	Rangers	34	22	8	4	85.27	52	Wardhaugh (Hearts)	30	Hearts	3	Celtic	1
1956–57	Rangers	34	26	3	5	96.48	55	Baird (Airdrieonians)	33	Falkirk	3	Kilmarnock	2
1957–58	Hearts	34	29	4	1	132.29	62	Wardhaugh (Hearts)	28	Clyde	1	Hibernian	0
1958–59	Rangers	34	21	8	5	92.51	50	Baker (Hibernian)	25	St. Mirren	3	Aberdeen	1
1959–60	Hearts	34	23	8	3	102.51	54	Baker (Hibernian)	42	Rangers	2	Kilmarnock	0
1960–61	Rangers	34	23	5	6	88.46	51	Harley (Third Lanark)	42	Dunfermline	2	Celtic	0
1961–62	Dundee	34	25	4	5	80.46	54	Gilzean (Dundee)	24	Rangers	2	St. Mirren	0
1962–63	Rangers	34	25	7	2	94.28	57	Millar (Rangers)	25	Rangers	4	Celtic	1
1963–64	Rangers	34	25	5	4	85.31	55	Gilzean (Dundee)	33	Rangers	3	Dundee	1
1964–65	Kilmarnock	34	22	6	6	62.33	50	Forrest (Rangers)	30	Celtic	3	Dunfermline	2
1965–66	Celtic	34	27	3	4	106.30	57	McBride (Celtic) Ferguson (Dunfermline)	31	Rangers	1	Celtic	0
1966–67	Celtic	34	26	6	2	111.33	58	Chalmers (Celtic)	24	Celtic	2	Aberdeen	0
1967–68	Celtic	34	30	3	1	106.24	63	Lennox (Celtic)	32	Dunfermline	3	Hearts	1
1968–69	Celtic	34	23	8	3	89.32	54	Cameron (Dundee United)	26	Celtic	4	Rangers	0
1969–70	Celtic	34	27	3	4	96.33	57	Stein (Rangers)	24	Aberdeen	3	Celtic	1
1970–71	Celtic	34	25	6	3	89.23	56	Busby (Airdrieonians)	20	Celtic	3	Rangers	2
1971–72	Celtic	34	28	4	2	96.28	60	Harper (Aberdeen)	33	Celtic	6	Hibernian	1
1972–73	Celtic	34	26	5	3	93.28	57	Gordon (Hibernian)	27	Rangers	3	Celtic	2
1973–74	Celtic	34	23	7	4	82.27	53	Deans (Celtic)	24	Celtic	3	Dundee United	0
1974–75	Rangers	34	25	6	3	86.33	56	Pettigrew (Motherwell) Gray (Dundee United)	20	Celtic	3	Airdrieonians	1
1975–76	Rangers	36	23	8	5	59.24	54	Dalglish (Celtic)	24	Rangers	3	Hearts	1
1976–77	Celtic	36	23	9	4	79.39	55	Pettigrew (Motherwell)	21	Celtic	1	Rangers	0
1977–78	Rangers	36	24	7	5	76.39	55	Johnstone (Rangers)	25	Rangers	2	Aberdeen	1
1978–79	Celtic	36	21	6	9	61.37	48	Ritchie (Morton)	22	Rangers	3	Hibernian	2
1979–80	Aberdeen	36	19	10	7	68.36	48	Somner (St. Mirren)	25	Celtic	1	Rangers	0
1980–81	Celtic	36	26	4	6	84.37	56	McGarvey (Celtic)	23	Rangers	4	Dundee United	1
1981–82	Celtic	36	24	7	5	79.33	55	McCluskey (Celtic)	20	Aberdeen	4	Rangers	1

ZLATKO VUJOVIC (Yugoslavia)

SPAIN

Season	Champion club	P	W	D	L	F.	A.	Pts.	Leading League Goalscorer		FA Cup Final			
1945–46	Sevilla CF	26	14	8	4	53.	37	36	Zarra (Athletic Bilbao)	24	Real Madrid	3	CF Valencia	1
1946–47	CF Valencia	26	16	2	8	54.	34	34	Zarra (Athletic Bilbao)	34	Real Madrid	2	RCD Espanol	0
1947–48	FC Barcelona	26	15	7	4	85.	31	37	Pahino (Celta, Vigo)	23	Sevilla CF	4	Real Celta	1
1948–49	FC Barcelona	26	16	5	5	66.	36	37	Cesar (FC Barcelona)	28	CF Valencia	1	Athletic Bilbao	0
1949–50	Atletico Madrid	26	15	3	8	71.	51	33	Zarra (Athletic Bilbao)	25	Athletic Bilbao	4	Valladolid	1
1950–51	Atletico Madrid	30	17	6	7	87.	50	40	Zarra (Athletic Bilbao)	36	FC Barcelona	3	Real Sociedad San Sebastian	0
1951–52	FC Barcelona	30	19	5	6	92.	43	43	Pahino (Real Madrid)	28	FC Barcelona	4	CF Valencia	2
1952–53	FC Barcelona	30	19	4	7	82.	43	42	Zarra (Athletic Bilbao)	24	FC Barcelona	2	Athletic Bilbao	1
1953–54	Real Madrid	30	17	6	7	72.	41	40	Di Stefano (Real Madrid)	29	CF Valencia	3	FC Barcelona	0
1954–55	Real Madrid	30	20	6	4	80.	31	46	Arza (Sevilla CF)	28	Athletic Bilbao	1	Sevilla CF	0
1955–56	Athletic Bilbao	30	22	4	4	79.	31	48	Di Stefano (Real Madrid)	24	Athletic Bilbao	2	Atletico Madrid	1
1956–57	Real Madrid	30	20	4	6	74.	35	44	Di Stefano (Real Madrid)	31	FC Barcelona	1	RCD Espanol	0
1957–58	Real Madrid	30	20	5	5	71.	26	45	Di Stefano (Real Madrid)	19	Athletic Bilbao	2	Real Madrid	0
1958–59	FC Barcelona	30	24	3	3	96.	26	51	Di Stefano (Real Madrid)	23	FC Barcelona	4	Granada	1
1959–60	FC Barcelona	30	22	2	6	86.	28	46	Puskas (Real Madrid)	26	Atletico Madrid	3	Real Madrid	1
1960–61	Real Madrid	30	24	4	2	89.	25	52	Puskas (Real Madrid)	27	Atletico Madrid	3	Real Madrid	2
1961–62	Real Madrid	30	19	5	6	58.	24	43	Seminario (Zaragoza)	25	Real Madrid	2	Sevilla CF	1
1962–63	Real Madrid	30	23	3	4	83.	33	49	Puskas (Real Madrid)	26	FC Barcelona	3	Zaragoza	1
1963–64	Real Madrid	30	22	2	6	61.	23	46	Puskas (Real Madrid)	20	Zaragoza	2	Atletico Madrid	1
1964–65	Real Madrid	30	21	5	4	64.	18	47	Re (FC Barcelona)	25	Atletico Madrid	1	Zaragoza	0
1965–66	Atletico Madrid	30	18	8	4	54.	20	44	Vava (Elche CF)	19	Zaragoza	2	Athletic Bilbao	1
1966–67	Real Madrid	30	19	9	2	58.	22	47	Waldo (CF Valencia)	26	CF Valencia	2	Athletic Bilbao	1
1967–68	Real Madrid	30	16	10	4	55.	26	42	Uriarte (Athletic Bilbao)	22	FC Barcelona	1	Real Madrid	0
1968–69	Real Madrid	30	18	11	1	46.	21	47	Amancio (Real Madrid) Garate (Atletico Madrid)	14	Athletic Bilbao	1	RCD Elche	0
1969–70	Atletico Madrid	30	18	6	6	53.	32	42	Amancio (Real Madrid) Garate (Atletico Madrid) Luis (Atletico Madrid)	16	Real Madrid	3	CF Valencia	1
1970–71	CF Valencia	30	18	7	5	41.	19	43	Garate (Atletico Madrid) Rexach (FC Barcelona)	17	FC Barcelona	4	CF Valencia	3
1971–72	Real Madrid	34	19	9	6	51.	27	47	Porta (Granada)	20	Atletico Madrid	2	CF Valencia	1
1972–73	Atletico Madrid	34	20	8	6	49.	29	48	Marianin (Oviedo)	19	Athletic Bilbao	2	FC Castellon	0
1973–74	FC Barcelona	34	21	8	5	75.	24	50	Quini (Sporting Gijon)	20	Real Madrid	4	FC Barcelona	0
1974–75	Real Madrid	34	20	10	4	66.	34	50	Carlos (Athletic Bilbao)	19	Real Madrid*	0	Atletico Madrid	0
1975–76	Real Madrid	34	20	8	6	54.	26	48	Quini (Sporting Gijon)	21	Atletico Madrid	1	Zaragoza	0
1976–77	Atletico Madrid	34	19	8	7	62.	33	46	Kempes (CF Valencia)	24	Real Betis*	2	Athletic Bilbao	2
1977–78	Real Madrid	34	22	3	9	77.	40	47	Kempes (CF Valencia)	28	FC Barcelona	3	Las Palmas	1
1978–79	Real Madrid	34	16	15	3	61.	36	47	Krankl (FC Barcelona)	29	CF Valencia	2	Real Madrid	0
1979–80	Real Madrid	34	22	9	3	70.	33	53	Quini (Sporting Gijon)	24	Real Madrid	6	CF Castilla	1

Season	Champion club	P	W	D	L	F.	A.	Pts	Leading League Goalscorer		FA Cup Final			
1980–81	Real Sociedad (San Sebastian)	34	19	7	8	52	29	45	Quini (FC Barcelona)	20	FC Barcelona	3	Sporting Gijon	1
1981–82	Real Sociedad (San Sebastian)	34	20	7	7	58	33	47	Quini (FC Barcelona)	26	Real Madrid	2	Sporting Gijon	1

KRANKL (Austria)

SWEDEN

Season	Champion club	P	W	D	L	F. A.	Pts	Leading League Goalscorer		FA Cup Final			
1945–46	IFK Norrkoping	22	16	3	3	67.22	35	Nordahl (Norrkping)	25	Malmo FF	3	Atvidaberg	0
1946–47	IFK Norrkoping	22	16	4	2	73.23	36	Gren (IFK Goteborg)	18	Malmo FF	3	AIK Stockholm	2
1947–48	IFK Norrkoping	22	15	3	4	56.32	33	Nordahl (Norrkoping)	17	Raa	6	Kenty	0
1948–49	Malmo FF	22	12	5	5	72.29	29	Franck (Halsingborg)	19	AIK Stockholm	1	Landskrona	0
1949–50	Malmo FF	22	20	2	0	82.21	42	Rydell (Malmo FF)	21	AIK Stockholm	3	Halsingborg	2
1950–51	Malmo FF	22	16	5	1	52.22	37	Jeppson (Djurgarden)	17	Malmo FF	2	Djurgarden	1
1951–52	IFK Norrkoping	22	15	5	2	50.21	35	Jacobsson (GAIS)	17	No competition			
1952–53	Malmo FF	22	14	3	5	60.32	31	Jacobsson (GAIS)	24	Malmo FF	3	IFK Norrkoping	2
1953–54	GAIS	22	10	7	5	46.39	27	Jacobsson (GAIS)	21	No competition (1953–54 to 1966)			
1954–55	Djurgarden	22	14	5	3	53.27	33	Hamrin (AIK Stockholm)	22				
1955–56	IFK Norrkoping	22	16	3	3	46.20	35	Bengtsson (Halmstad)	22				
1956–57	IFK Norrkoping	22	17	1	4	64.25	35	Johannson (IFK Goteborg)	27				
1957–58	IFK Goteborg	33	22	3	8	92.49	47	Kallgren (Norrkoping)	27				
1959	Djurgarden	22	11	10	1	46.20	32	Borjesson (Orgryte)	21				
1960	IFK Norrkoping	22	17	4	1	75.26	38	Borjesson (Orgryte)	24				
1961	Elfsborg	22	13	5	4	54.37	31	Johansson (IFK Goteborg)	20				
1962	IFK Norrkoping	22	14	4	4	39.19	32	Skiold (Djurgarden)	21				
1963	IFK Norrkoping	22	12	7	3	47.30	31	Larsson (Malmo FF) Heineman (Degerfors)	17				
1964	Djurgarden	22	13	5	4	46.20	31	Granbom (Halsingborg)	22				
1965	Malmo FF	22	15	4	3	64.24	34	Larsson (Malmo FF)	28				
1966	Djurgarden	22	15	3	4	46.17	33	Kindvall (Norrkoping)	20				
1967	Malmo FF	22	14	5	3	53.21	33	Szepanski (Malmo FF)	22	Malmo FF	2	IFK Norrkoping	0
1968	Oster IFK	22	12	3	7	44.28	27	Eklund (Atvidaberg)	17	No competition			
1969	IFK Goteborg	22	13	5	4	36.19	31	Almqvist (IFK Goteborg)	16	IFK Norrkoping	1	AIK Stockholm	0
1970	Malmo FF	22	11	7	4	30.20	29	Larsson (Malmo FF)	16	Atvidaberg	2	Sandviken	0
1971	Malmo FF	22	12	6	4	46.22	30	Sandberg (Atvidaberg)	17	Atvidaberg	3	Malmo FF	2
1972	Atvidaberg	22	15	3	4	65.22	33	Edstrom (Atvidaberg) Sandberg (Atvidaberg)	16	Landskrona	3	IFK Norrkoping	2
1973	Atvidaberg	26	16	5	5	53.34	37	Mattsson (Oster IFK)	20	Malmo FF	7	Atvidaberg	0
1974	Malmo FF	26	19	5	2	48.15	43	Mattsson (Oster IFK)	19	Malmo FF	2	Oster IFK	0
1975	Malmo FF	26	18	6	2	53.17	42	Mattsson (Oster IFK)	31	Malmo FF	1	Djurgarden	0
1976	Halmstad BK	26	17	4	5	56.27	38	Backe (Halmstad BK)	21	AIK Stockholm	4	Landskrona	1
1977	Malmo FF	26	15	8	3	41.19	38	Almqvist (IFK Goteborg) Aronsson (Landskrona)	15	Oster IFK	1	Hammarby BK	0
1978	Oster IFK	26	15	8	3	46.20	38	Berggren (Djurdgarden)	19	Malmo FF	2	Kalmar FF	0
1979	Halmstad BK	26	12	12	2	38.21	36	Werner (Hammarby BK)	14	IFK Goteborg	6	Atvidaberg	1
1980	Oster IFK	26	13	11	2	41. 16	37	Ohlsson (Hammerby BK)	19	Malmo FF*	3	Kalmar FF	3
1981	Oster IFK	26	19	2	5	57.20	40	Nilsson (IFK Goteborg)	20	Kalmar FF	4	Elfsborg	0
1982										IFK Goteborg	3	Oster IFK	2

PASARELLA (Argentina)

SWITZERLAND

Season	Champion club	P	W	D	L	F. A.	Pts.	Leading League Goalscorer		FA Cup Final			
1945–46	Servette	26	16	4	6	55.36	36	Friedlander (Grasshoppers)	25	Grasshoppers	3	Lausanne	0
1946–47	FC Biel	26	14	8	4	50.32	36	Amado (Grasshoppers) Blaser (Young Boys)	19	FC Basle	3	Lausanne	0
1947–48	Bellinzona	26	15	8	3	58.28	38	Righetti I (FC Grenchen)	26	Chaux de Fonds	8	FC Grenchen	4
1948–49	Lugano	26	18	4	4	41.18	40	Fatton (Servette)	21	Servette	3	Grasshoppers	0
1949–50	Servette	26	16	3	7	73.41	45	Fatton (Servette)	32	Lausanne	5	Cantonal	1
1950–51	Lausanne	26	14	6	6	58.31	34	Friedlander (Lausanne)	22	Chaux de Fonds	3	FC Locarno	2
1951–52	Grasshoppers	26	16	6	4	79.38	38	Hugi II (FC Basle)	24	Grasshoppers	2	FC Lugano	0
1952–53	FC Basle	26	17	8	1	72.38	42	Hugi II (FC Basle) Meier (Young Boys)	32	Young Boys	4	Grasshoppers	2
1953–54	Chaux de Fonds	26	20	2	4	78.36	42	Hugi II (FC Basle)	29	Chaux de Fonds	2	FC Fribourg	0
1954–55	Chaux de Fonds	26	19	4	3	99.46	42	Mauron (Chaux de Fonds)	30	Chaux de Fonds	3	FC Thun	1
1955–56	Grasshoppers	26	19	4	3	94.36	42	Vukosaljevic (Grasshoppers)	33	Grasshoppers	1	Young Boys	0
1956–57	Young Boys, Berne	26	21	3	2	76.22	45	Kauer (Chaux de Fonds)	29	Chaux de Fonds	3	Lausanne	1
1957–58	Young Boys, Berne	26	20	3	3	76.37	43	Wechselberger (Young Boys)	22	Young Boys	5	Grasshoppers	2
1958–59	Young Boys, Berne	26	16	6	4	79.42	38	Meier (Young Boys)	24	FC Grenchen	1	Servette	0
1959–60	Young Boys, Berne	26	20	2	4	86.44	42	Schneider (Young Boys)	25	FC Lucerne	1	FC Grenchen	0
1960–61	Servette	26	23	0	3	77.29	46	Robbiani (Grasshoppers)	27	Chaux de Fonds	1	FC Biel	0
1961–62	Servette	26	18	4	4	93.30	40	Fatton (Servette)	25	Lausanne	4	Bellinzona	0
1962–63	FC Zurich	26	20	4	2	81.33	44	Von Burg (FC Zurich)	24	FC Basle	2	Grasshoppers	0
1963–64	Chaux de Fonds	26	17	5	4	68.36	39	Desbiolles (Servette)	23	Lausanne	2	Chaux de Fonds	0
1964–65	Lausanne	26	15	6	5	61.32	36	Blattler (Grasshoppers) Kerkhoffs (Lausanne)	19	FC Sion	2	Servette	1
1965–66	FC Zurich	26	18	6	2	73.25	42	Blattler (Grasshoppers)	28	FC Zurich	2	Servette	0
1966–67	FC Basle	26	16	8	2	61.20	40	Blattler (Grasshoppers) Künzli (FC Zurich)	24	FC Basle	2	Lausanne	1
1967–68	FC Zurich	26	16	6	4	63.27	38	Künzli (FC Zurich)	28	FC Lugano	2	Winterthur	1
1968–69	FC Basle	26	13	10	3	48.28	36	Peters (FC Biel)	24	St. Gallen	2	Bellinzona	0
1969–70	FC Basle	26	15	7	4	59.23	37	Künzli (FC Zurich)	19	FC Zurich	4	FC Basle	1
1970–71	Grasshoppers	26	20	2	4	59.21	42	Müller (W) (Young Boys)	19	Servette	2	FC Lugano	0
1971–72	FC Basle	26	18	7	1	66.28	43	Dimmeler (Winterthur) Dörfel (Servette)	17	FC Zurich	1	FC Basle	0
1972–73	FC Basle	26	17	5	4	57.30	39	Grahn (Lausanne) Hitzfeld (FC Basle)	18	FC Zurich	2	FC Basle	0
1973–74	FC Zurich	26	20	5	1	67.20	45	Jeandupeux (FC Zurich)	22	FC Sion	3	Xamax (Neuchatel)	2
1974–75	FC Zurich	26	19	1	6	63.19	39	Katic (FC Zurich)	23	FC Basle	2	Winterthur	1
1975–76	FC Zurich	26	19	6	1	69.26	44	Risi (FC Zurich)	33	FC Zurich	1	Servette	0
1976–77	FC Basle	32	19	7	6	73.46	45	Cucinotta (FC Zurich)	28	Young Boys	1	St. Gallen	0
1977–78	Grasshoppers	32	19	8	5	77.39	46	Künzli (Lausanne)	20	Servette	3	Grasshoppers	2
1978–79	Servette	32	22	6	4	79.28	50	Risi (FC Zurich)	16	Servette	4	Young Boys	3

Season	Champion club	P	W	D	L	F. A.	Pts	Leading League Goalscorer		FA Cup Final			
1979–80	FC Basle	36	21	9	6	91.38	51	Sulser (Grasshoppers)	25	FC Sion	2	Young Boys	1
1980–81	FC Zurich	26	18	4	4	59.29	40	Risi (FC Lucerne)	18	Lausanne	4	FC Zurich	3
1981–82	Grasshoppers	30	21	7	2	72.24	49	Sulser (Grasshoppers)	22	FC Sion	1	FC Basle	0

TARDELLI (Italy)

WALES

Season	Champion club	P	W	D	L	F. A.	Pts.	Leading League Goalscorer	FA Cup Final			
1945–46	Lovells Athletic	36	31	3	2	171.43	65		No competition			
1946–47	Lovells Athletic	38	26	8	4	135.36	60		Chester City	5	Merthyr Tydfil	1
1947–48	Lovells Athletic	38	25	8	5	116.35	58		Lovells Athletic	3	Shrewsbury Town	0
1948–49	Merthyr Tydfil	36	26	5	5	108.37	57		Merthyr Tydfil	2	Swansea Town	0
1949–50	Merthyr Tydfil	38	28	5	5	113.49	61		Swansea Town	4	Wrexham	1
1950–51	Swansea Town Reserves	38	25	6	7	103.53	56		Merthyr Tydfil	4	Cardiff City	3
1951–52	Merthyr Tydfil	36	26	4	6	118.63	56		Rhyl	4	Merthyr Tydfil	3
1952–53	Ebbw Vale & CWM	38	30	5	3	126.36	65		Rhyl	2	Chester City	1
1953–54	Pembroke Borough	38	25	3	10	117.90	53		Flint Town Utd	2	Chester City	0
1954–55	Newport County Reserves	38	25	3	10	117.90	53		Flint Town Utd	2	Chester City	0
1955–56	Pembroke Borough	38	25	6	7	124.56	56		Cardiff City	3	Swansea Town	2
1956–57	Haverfordwest County	38	22	7	9	97.53	51		Wrexham	2	Swansea Town	1
1957–58	Ton Pentre	38	22	6	10	110.80	50		Wrexham	3	Chester City	2
1958–59	Abergavenny Thursday	36	28	4	4	112.37	60		Cardiff City	2	Lovells Athletic	0
1959–60	Abergavenny Thursday	38	30	5	3	126.39	65		Wrexham	1	Cardiff City	0
1960–61	Ton Pentre	38	27	6	5	137.34	60		Swansea Town	3	Bangor City	1
1961–62	Swansea Town Reserves	38	27	6	5	123.44	60		Bangor City	3	Wrexham	1
1962–63	Swansea Town Reserves	38	33	2	3	124.30	68		Borough United	2	Newport County	1
1963–64	Swansea Town Reserves	34	23	10	1	110.36	56	No records	Cardiff City	5	Bangor City	3
1964–65	Swansea Town Reserves	30	21	6	3	88.27	48		Cardiff City	8	Wrexham	2
1965–66	Lovells Athletic	30	24	5	1	80.23	53		Swansea Town	2	Chester City	1
1966–67	Cardiff City Reserves	30	20	4	6	88.34	44		Cardiff City	2	Wrexham	1
1967–68	Cardiff City Reserves	34	25	6	3	136.45	56		Cardiff City	6	Hereford United	1
1968–69	Bridgend Town	34	25	5	4	87.30	55		Cardiff City	5	Swansea Town	1
1969–70	Cardiff City Reserves	34	25	8	1	106.35	58		Cardiff City	5	Chester City	0
1970–71	Llanelli	34	25	6	3	73.22	56		Cardiff City	4	Wrexham	1
1971–72	Cardiff City Reserves	34	23	6	5	94.24	52		Wrexham	3	Cardiff City	2
1972–73	Bridgend Town	34	25	5	4	91.33	55		Cardiff City	5	Bangor City	1
1973–74	Ton Pentre	34	21	8	5	77.33	50		Cardiff City	3	Stourbridge Town	0
1974–75	Newport County Reserves	34	19	13	2	62.29	51		Wrexham	5	Cardiff City	2
1975–76	Swansea City Reserves	34	22	7	5	91.32	51		Cardiff City	6	Hereford United	5
1976–77	Llanelli	34	24	5	5	69.36	53		Shrewsbury Town	4	Cardiff City	2
1977–78	Llanelli	34	23	8	3	63.20	54		Wrexham	3	Bangor City	1
1978–79	Pontllanfraith	34	23	7	4	73.37	53		Shrewsbury Town	2	Wrexham	1
1979–80	Newport County Reserves	34	22	8	4	102.39	52		Newport County	5	Shrewsbury Town	1
1980–81	Haverfordwest County	34	19	10	5	61.39	48		Swansea City	2	Hereford United	1
1981–82	Ton Pentre	34	21	7	6	84.46	70		Swansea City	2	Cardiff City	1

CUETO (Peru)

The History of the European Championship

1960. Winners: (Russia)

Preliminary round:

Eire 2 Czechoslovakia 0

Czechoslovakia 4 Eire 0

First round:

Russia 3 Hungary 1
Hungary 0 Russia 1
Poland 2 Spain 4
Spain 3 Poland 0
Denmark 2 Czechoslovakia 2
Czechoslovakia 5 Denmark 1
Romania 3 Turkey 0
Turkey 2 Romania 0

Norway 0 Austria 1
Austria 5 Norway 2
France 7 Greece 1
Greece 1 France 1
Portugal 2 East Germany 0
East Germany 2 Portugal 3
Yugoslavia 2 Bulgaria 0
Bulgaria 1 Yugoslavia 1

Quarter finals:

Russia v Spain—Spain withdrew
France 5 Austria 2
Austria 2 France 4
Romania 0 Czechoslovakia 2
Czechoslovakia 3 Romania 0
Portugal 2 Yugoslavia 1
Yugoslavia 5 Portugal 1

Final stages in France.

Semi-finals:
Paris.

France 4 — Yugoslavia 5
Heutte (2), Vincent, Wisnieski. — Galic, Zanetic, Knez, Jerkovic (2)

France: Lamia; Wendling, Rodzik; Marcel, Herbin, Ferrier; Heutte, Muller, Wisnieski, Stievenard, Vincent.

Yugoslavia: Soskic; Durkovic, Jusufi; Zanetic, Zebec, Perusic; Knez, Jerkovic, Galic, Sekularac, Kostic.

Marseille.
Russia 3 — Czechoslovakia 0
Ivanov (2), Ponedelnik

Russia: Yachin; Tchokeli, Krutikov; Vojnov, Maslenkin, Netto; Metreveli, Ivanov, Ponedelnik, Babukin, Meschki.

Czechoslovakia: Schroif; Safranek, Novak; Bubernik, Popluhar, Masopust; Vojta, Moravcik, Kvasnak, Bubnik, Dolinsky.

Paris.

Final.

Russia 2 — Yugoslavia 1 (After Extra Time).
Metreveli, Ponedelnik — Galic

Russia: Yachin; Tchokeli, Krutikov; Vojnov, Maslenkin, Netto; Metreveli, Ivanov, Ponedelnik, Babukin, Meschki.

Yugoslavia: Vidinic; Durkovic, Jusufi; Zanetic, Miladinovic, Perusic; Matus, Jerkovic, Galic, Sekularac, Kostic.

Marseille.

Play-off for Third Place.

Czechoslovakia 2 — France 0
Pavlovic, Bubnik

Czechoslovakia: Schroif; Safranek, Novak; Bubernik, Popluhar, Masopust; Pavlovic, Vojta, Molnar, Bubnik, Dolinsky.

France: Taillandier; Rodzik, Chorda; Marcel, Jonquet, Siatka; Heutte, Douis, Wisnieski, Stievenard, Vincent.

1964. Winners: (Spain)

First round:

Byes: Luxembourg, Austria, Russia.

Spain 6 Romania 0
Romania 3 Spain 1
Poland 0 N. Ireland 2
N. Ireland 2 Poland 0
Eire 4 Iceland 2
Iceland 1 Eire 1

Hungary 3 Wales 1
Wales 1 Hungary 1
East Germany 2 Czechoslovakia 1
Czechoslovakia 1 East Germany 1
England 1 France 1
France 5 England 2

Holland 3 Switzerland 1
Switzerland 1 Holland 1
Norway 0 Sweden 2
Sweden 1 Norway 1
Italy 6 Turkey 0
Turkey 1 Italy 0

1964 (First round, continued)

Greece v Albania—Greece withdrew

Denmark 6 Malta 1
Malta 1 Denmark 3
Yugoslavia 3 Belgium 2
Belgium 0 Yugoslavia 1

Bulgaria 3 Portugal 1
Portugal 3 Bulgaria 1

Play-off in Rome:

Bulgaria 1 Portugal 0

Second round:

N. Ireland 1 Spain 1
Spain 1 N. Ireland 0
Austria 0 Eire 0
Eire 3 Austria 2
Hungary 2 East Germany 1
East Germany 3 Hungary 3
France 3 Bulgaria 1
Bulgaria 1 France 0

Holland 1 Luxembourg 1
Holland 1 Luxembourg 2
NB (Both games were played in Holland!)
Denmark 4 Albania 0
Albania 1 Denmark 0
Yugoslavia 0 Sweden 0
Sweden 3 Yugoslavia 2
Russia 2 Italy 0
Italy 1 Russia 1

Quarter-finals:

France 1 Hungary 3
Hungary 2 France 1

Spain 5 Eire 1
Eire 0 Spain 2

Sweden 1 Russia 1
Russia 3 Sweden 1

Luxembourg 3 Denmark 3
Denmark 2 Luxembourg 2

Play-off in Amsterdam:

Denmark 1 Luxembourg 0

Final stages in Spain.

Semi-finals:

Barcelona.

Russia 3 Denmark 0
Ivanov, Voronin, Ponedelnik

Russia: Yachin; Mudrik, Glotov; Anitchkin, Schesternev, Voronin; Chislenko, Ivanov, Ponedelnik, Gusarov, Choussainov.

Denmark: Nielsen (L); Hansen (J), Hansen (K); Hansen (B), Larsen, Nielsen (E); Berthelsen, Thorst, Madsen, Soerensen, Danielsen.

Madrid.

Spain 2 Hungary 1 (After extra time).
Pereda, Amancio Nagy

Spain: Iribar; Rivilla, Calleja; Zoco, Olivella, Fuste; Amancio, Pereda, Marcelino, Suarez, Lapetra.

Hungary: Szentmihalyi; Matrai, Sarosi; Nagy, Meszoly, Sipos; Bene, Komora, Albert, Tichy, Fenyvesi.

Madrid.

Final.

Spain 2 Russia 1
Pereda, Marcelino Choussainov

Spain: Iribar; Rivilla, Calleja; Zoco, Olivella, Fuste; Amancio, Pereda, Marcelino, Suarez, Lapetra.

Russia: Yachin; Schustikov, Mudrik; Anitchkin, Schesternev, Voronin; Chislenko, Ivanov, Ponedelnik, Kornejev, Choussainov.

Barcelona.

Play-off for Third Place.

Hungary 3 Denmark 1 (After extra time).
Novak (2), Bene Berthelsen

Hungary: Szentmihalyi; Novak, Ihasz; Solymosi, Meszoly, Sipos; Farkas, Varga, Albert, Bene, Fenyvesi.

Denmark: Nielsen (L); Wolmar, Hansen (K); Hansen (B), Larsen, Nielsen (E); Berthelsen, Soerensen, Madsen, Thorst, Nielsen (D).

1968. Winners: (Italy)

Qualifying round.

Group 1.

Spain 2 Eire 0
Eire 0 Spain 0
Spain 2 Turkey 0
Turkey 0 Spain 0
Spain 2 Czechoslovakia 1
Czechoslovakia 1 Spain 0
Czechoslovakia 3 Turkey 0
Turkey 0 Czechoslovakia 0
Eire 0 Czechoslovakia 2
Czechoslovakia 1 Eire 2
Eire 2 Turkey 1
Turkey 2 Eire 1

	P	W	D	L	F.	A.	Pts
Spain	6	3	2	1	6.	2	8
Czechoslovakia	6	3	1	2	8.	4	7
Eire	6	2	1	3	5.	8	5
Turkey	6	1	2	3	3.	8	4

Jurkemik (Czechoslavkia (5)) beats Klaus Fischer (West Germany) in 1980

Group 2.

Portugal 1 Sweden 2
Sweden 1 Portugal 1
Norway 1 Portugal 2
Portugal 2 Norway 1
Sweden 5 Norway 2
Norway 3 Sweden 1
Sweden 0 Bulgaria 2
Bulgaria 3 Sweden 0
Bulgaria 4 Norway 2
Norway 0 Bulgaria 0
Portugal 0 Bulgaria 0
Bulgaria 1 Portugal 0

	P	W	D	L	F. A.	Pts
Bulgaria	6	4	2	0	10. 2	10
Portugal	6	2	2	2	6. 6	6
Sweden	6	2	1	3	9.12	5
Norway	6	1	1	4	9.14	3

Group 3.

Russia 4 Austria 3
Austria 1 Russia 0
Greece 0 Russia 1
Russia 4 Greece 0
Austria 2 Finland 1
Finland 0 Austria 0
Greece 2 Finland 1
Finland 1 Greece 1
Russia 2 Finland 0
Finland 2 Russia 5
Greece 4 Austria 1
Austria 1 Greece 1

	P	W	D	L	F. A.	Pts
Russia	6	5	0	1	16. 6	10
Greece	6	2	2	2	8. 9	6
Austria	6	2	2	2	8.10	6
Finland	6	0	2	4	5.12	2

Group 4.

West Germany 6 Albania 0
Albania 0 West Germany 0
Yugoslavia 1 West Germany 0
West Germany 3 Yugoslavia 1
Yugoslavia 4 Albania 0
Albania 0 Yugoslavia 2

	P	W	D	L	F. A.	Pts
Yugoslavia	4	3	0	1	8. 3	6
West Germany	4	2	1	1	9. 2	5
Albania	4	0	1	3	0.12	1

Group 5.

East Germany 4 Holland 3
Holland 1 East Germany 0
Hungary 2 Holland 1
Holland 2 Hungary 2
Hungary 3 East Germany 1
East Germany 1 Hungary 0
Hungary 6 Denmark 0
Denmark 0 Hungary 2
East Germany 3 Denmark 2
Denmark 1 East Germany 1
Holland 2 Denmark 0
Denmark 3 Holland 2

	P	W	D	L	F. A.	Pts
Hungary	6	4	1	1	15. 5	9
East Germany	6	3	1	2	10.10	7
Holland	6	2	1	3	11.11	5
Denmark	6	1	1	4	6.16	3

Group 6.

Switzerland 2 Italy 2
Italy 4 Switzerland 0
Italy 5 Cyprus 0
Cyprus 0 Italy 2
Romania 4 Switzerland 2
Switzerland 7 Romania 1
Romania 0 Italy 1
Italy 3 Romania 1
Romania 7 Cyprus 0
Cyprus 1 Romania 5
Switzerland 5 Cyprus 0
Cyprus 2 Switzerland 1

	P	W	D	L	F. A.	Pts
Italy	6	5	1	0	17. 3	11
Romania	6	3	0	3	18.14	6
Switzerland	6	2	1	3	17.13	5
Cyprus	6	1	0	5	3.25	2

1968 (Continued)

Group 7.

Poland 4 Luxembourg 0
Luxembourg 0 Poland 0
France 2 Poland 1
Poland 1 France 4
Belgium 3 Luxembourg 0
Luxembourg 0 Belgium 5
Belgium 2 France 1
France 1 Belgium 1
France 3 Luxembourg 1
Luxembourg 0 France 3
Poland 3 Belgium 1
Belgium 2 Poland 4

	P	W	D	L	F. A.	Pts
France	6	4	1	1	14. 6	9
Belgium	6	3	1	2	14. 9	7
Poland	6	3	1	2	13. 9	7
Luxembourg	6	0	1	5	1.18	1

Group 8.

N. Ireland 0 England 2
England 2 N. Ireland 0
Scotland 2 N. Ireland 1
N. Ireland 1 Scotland 0
England 5 Wales 1
Wales 0 England 3
Wales 1 Scotland 1
Scotland 3 Wales 2
England 2 Scotland 3
Scotland 1 England 1
N. Ireland 0 Wales 0
Wales 2 N. Ireland 0

	P	W	D	L	F. A.	Pts
England	6	4	1	1	15. 5	9
Scotland	6	3	2	1	10. 8	8
Wales	6	1	2	3	6.12	4
N. Ireland	6	1	1	4	2. 8	3

Quarter finals.

Bulgaria 3 Italy 2
Italy 2 Bulgaria 0

France 1 Yugoslavia 1
Yugoslavia 5 France 1

England 1 Spain 0
Spain 1 England 2

Hungary 2 Russia 0
Russia 3 Hungary 0

Final stages in Italy.

Semi-finals:

Naples.

Italy 0 Russia 0 (After extra time).
Italy won the toss.

Italy: Zoff; Burgnich, Facchetti; Bercellino, Castano, Ferrini; Domenghini, Juliano, Mazzola, Rivera, Prati.

Russia: Pshenichnikov; Afonin, Istomin; Kaplichniy, Schesternev, Lenev; Malofeev, Bichovets, Banishevski, Logofet, Evruzkhin.

Florence.

Yugoslavia 1 England 0
Dzajic

Yugoslavia: Pantelic; Fazlagic, Damjanovic; Pavlovic, Paunovic, Holcer; Petkovic, Osim, Musemic, Trivic, Dzajic.

England: Banks; Newton, Wilson; Mullery, Labone, Moore; Ball, Peters, Charlton (R), Hunt, Hunter.

Rome.

Play-off for Third Place.

England 2 Russia 0
Hurst, Charlton (R)

England: Banks; Wright, Wilson; Stiles, Labone, Moore; Hunter, Hunt, Hurst, Charlton (R), Peters.

Russia: Pschenichnikov; Afonin, Istomin; Kaplichniy, Schesternev, Lenev; Malofeev, Bichovets, Banishevski, Logofet, Evruzkhin.

Final.

Rome.

Italy 1 — Yugoslavia 1 (After extra time).
Domenghini — Dzajic

Italy: Zoff; Burgnich, Facchetti; Ferrini, Guarneri, Castano; Domenghini, Juliano, Anastasi, Lodetti, Prati.

Yugoslavia: Pantelic; Fazlagic, Damjanovic; Pavlovic, Paunovic, Holcer; Petkovic, Trivic, Musemic, Acimovic, Dzajic.

Rome.

Final (Re-play).

Italy 2 — Yugoslavia 0
Riva, Anastasi

Italy: Zoff; Burgnich, Facchetti; Rosato, Guarneri, Salvadore; Domenghini, Mazzola, Anastasi, De Sisti, Riva.

Yugoslavia: Pantelic; Fazlagic, Damjanovic; Pavlovic, Paunovic, Holcer; Hosic, Trivic, Musemic, Acimovic, Dzajic.

Panenka (with moustache), whose brilliantly taken penalty won the 1976 title for Czechoslovakia.

Sandro Mazzola who helped Italy win the European Championship in 1968.

1972. Winners (West Germany)

Qualifying round.

Group 1.

Czechoslovakia 1 Finland 1
Finland 0 Czechoslovakia 4
Wales 3 Finland 0
Finland 0 Wales 1
Romania 2 Wales 0
Wales 0 Romania 0
Romania 3 Finland 0
Finland 0 Romania 4
Czechoslovakia 1 Romania 0
Romania 2 Czechoslovakia 1
Czechoslovakia 1 Wales 0
Wales 1 Czechoslovakia 3

	P	W	D	L	F.	A.	Pts
Romania	6	4	1	1	11.	2	9
Czechoslovakia	6	4	1	1	11.	4	9
Wales	6	2	1	3	5.	6	5
Finland	6	0	1	5	1.	16	1

Group 2.

Hungary 2 Bulgaria 0
Bulgaria 3 Hungary 0
Hungary 1 France 1
France 0 Hungary 2
Norway 1 Hungary 3
Hungary 4 Norway 0
Bulgaria 2 France 1
France 2 Bulgaria 1
Norway 1 Bulgaria 4
Bulgaria 1 Norway 1
France 3 Norway 1
Norway 1 France 3

	P	W	D	L	F.	A.	Pts
Hungary	6	4	1	1	12.	5	9
Bulgaria	6	3	1	2	11.	7	7
France	6	3	1	2	10.	8	7
Norway	6	0	1	5	5.	18	1

Group 3.

England 1 Switzerland 1
Switzerland 2 England 3
England 3 Greece 0
Greece 0 England 2
England 5 Malta 0
Malta 0 England 1
Greece 0 Switzerland 1
Switzerland 1 Greece 0
Switzerland 5 Malta 0
Malta 1 Switzerland 2
Malta 1 Greece 1
Greece 2 Malta 0

	P	W	D	L	F.	A.	Pts
England	6	5	1	0	15.	3	11
Switzerland	6	4	1	1	12.	5	9
Greece	6	1	1	4	3.	8	3
Malta	6	0	1	5	2.	16	1

Group 4.

Russia 2 Spain 1
Spain 0 Russia 0
N. Ireland 1 Russia 1
Russia 1 N. Ireland 0
Cyprus 1 Russia 3
Russia 6 Cyprus 1
Spain 3 N. Ireland 0
N. Ireland 1 Spain 1
Spain 7 Cyprus 0
Cyprus 0 Spain 2
N. Ireland 5 Cyprus 0
Cyprus 0 N. Ireland 3

	P	W	D	L	F.	A.	Pts
Russia	6	4	2	0	13.	4	10
Spain	6	3	2	1	14.	3	8
N. Ireland	6	2	2	2	10.	6	6
Cyprus	6	0	0	6	2.	26	0

Group 5.

Belgium 3 Portugal 0
Portugal 1 Belgium 1
Belgium 3 Scotland 0
Scotland 1 Belgium 0
Belgium 2 Denmark 0
Denmark 1 Belgium 2
Portugal 2 Scotland 0
Scotland 2 Portugal 1
Portugal 5 Denmark 0
Denmark 0 Portugal 1
Scotland 1 Denmark 0
Denmark 1 Scotland 0

	P	W	D	L	F.	A.	Pts
Belgium	6	4	1	1	11.	3	9
Portugal	6	3	1	2	10.	6	7
Scotland	6	3	0	3	4.	7	6
Denmark	6	1	0	5	2.	11	2

1972 (continued)

Group 6.

Austria 1 Italy 2
Italy 2 Austria 2
Italy 3 Sweden 0
Sweden 0 Italy 0
Italy 3 Eire 0
Eire 1 Italy 2
Sweden 1 Austria 0
Austria 1 Sweden 0
Eire 1 Austria 4
Austria 6 Eire 0
Eire 1 Sweden 1
Sweden 1 Eire 0

	P	W	D	L	F. A.	Pts
Italy	6	4	2	0	12. 4	10
Austria	6	3	1	2	14. 6	7
Sweden	6	2	2	2	3. 5	6
Eire	6	0	1	5	3.17	1

Group 7.

Yugoslavia 2 Holland 0
Holland 1 Yugoslavia 1
Yugoslavia 0 East Germany 0
East Germany 1 Yugoslavia 2
Yugoslavia 0 Luxembourg 0
Luxembourg 0 Yugoslavia 2
Holland 3 East Germany 2
East Germany 1 Holland 0
Holland 6 Luxembourg 0
Luxembourg 0 Holland 8
East Germany 2 Luxembourg 1
Luxembourg 0 East Germany 5

	P	W	D	L	F. A.	Pts
Yugoslavia	6	3	3	0	7. 2	9
Holland	6	3	1	2	18. 6	7
East Germany	6	3	1	2	11. 6	7
Luxembourg	6	0	1	5	1.23	1

Group 8.

West Germany 0 Poland 0
Poland 1 West Germany 3
West Germany 1 Turkey 1
Turkey 0 West Germany 3
West Germany 2 Albania 0
Albania 0 West Germany 1
Poland 5 Turkey 1
Turkey 1 Poland 0
Poland 3 Albania 0
Albania 1 Poland 1
Turkey 2 Albania 1
Albania 3 Turkey 0

	P	W	D	L	F. A.	Pts
West Germany	6	4	2	0	10. 2	10
Poland	6	2	2	2	10. 6	6
Turkey	6	2	1	3	5.13	5
Albania	6	1	1	4	5. 9	3

Quarter-finals.

England 1 West Germany 3
West Germany 0 England 0

Italy 0 Belgium 0
Belgium 2 Italy 1

Yugoslavia 0 Russia 0
Russia 3 Yugoslavia 0

Hungary 1 Romania 1
Romania 2 Hungary 2

Play-off in Belgrade:

Hungary 2 Romania 1

Final stages in Belgium.

Semi-finals:

Brussels.

Russia 1 — Hungary 0
Konkov

Russia: Rudakov; Dzodzuashvili, Istomin; Kaplichniy, Churtsilava, Troshkin; Baidatschni, Kolotov, Banishevski (Nodija), Konkov, Onitschenko.

Hungary: Geczi; Fabian, Juhasz (P); Juhasz (J), Balint, Pancsics; Szoke, Kocsis (Dunai), Bene (Albert), Ku, Zambo.

Antwerp.

Belgium 1 — West Germany 2
Polleunis — Müller (2)

Belgium: Piot; Heylens, Dolmans; Dockx, Van den Daele, Thissen; Semmeling, Verheyen, Lambert, Van Himst, Maertens (Polleunis).

West Germany: Maier; Höttges, Breitner; Schwarzenbeck, Beckenbauer, Wimmer; Heynckes, Hoeness (Grabowski), Müller, Netzer, Kremers (E).

Belgium's Rene Van der Eycken in a heading duel against England in 1980.

1972 (continued)

Brussels.

Final.

West Germany 3 Russia 0
Müller (2), Wimmer
West Germany: Maier; Höttges, Breitner; Schwarzenbeck, Beckenbauer, Wimmer; Heynckes, Hoeness, Müller, Netzer, Kremers (E).
Russia: Rudakov; Dzodzuashvili, Istomin; Kaplichniy, Churtsilava, Troshkin; Baidatschni, Kolotov, Banishevski (Kosinkevitsch), Konkov (Dolmatov), Onitschenko.

Liège.

Play-off for Third Place.

Belgium 2 Hungary 1
Lambert, Van Himst Ku (Pen)
Belgium: Piot; Heylens, Dolmans; Dockx, Van den Daele, Thissen; Semmeling, Verheyen, Lambert, Van Himst, Polleunis.
Hungary: Geczi; Fabian, Juhasz (P); Juhasz (J), Balint, Pancsics; Kozma, Albert, Dunai, Ku, Zambo (Szucs).

1976. Winners (Czechoslovakia)

Qualifying round

Group 1.

England 3 Czechoslovakia 0
Czechoslovakia 2 England 1
Czechoslovakia 5 Portugal 0
Portugal 1 Czechoslovakia 1
Czechoslovakia 4 Cyprus 0
Cyprus 0 Czechoslovakia 3
England 0 Portugal 0
Portugal 1 England 1
England 5 Cyprus 0
Cyprus 0 England 1
Portugal 1 Cyprus 0
Cyprus 0 Portugal 2

	P	W	D	L	F. A.	Pts
Czechoslovakia	6	4	1	1	15. 5	9
England	6	3	2	1	11. 3	8
Portugal	6	2	3	1	5. 7	7
Cyprus	6	0	0	6	0.16	0

Group 2,

Wales 2 Hungary 0
Hungary 1 Wales 2
Wales 1 Austria 0
Austria 2 Wales 1
Wales 5 Luxembourg 0
Luxembourg 1 Wales 3
Hungary 2 Austria 1
Austria 0 Hungary 0
Hungary 8 Luxembourg 1
Luxembourg 2 Hungary 4
Austria 6 Luxembourg 2
Luxembourg 1 Austria 2

	P	W	D	L	F. A.	Pts
Wales	6	5	0	1	14. 4	10
Hungary	6	3	1	2	15. 8	7
Austria	6	3	1	2	11. 7	7
Luxembourg	6	0	0	6	7.28	0

Group 3.

Yugoslavia 1 N. Ireland 0
N. Ireland 1 Yugoslavia 0
Yugoslavia 3 Sweden 0
Sweden 1 Yugoslavia 2
Yugoslavia 3 Norway 1
Norway 1 Yugoslavia 3
Sweden 0 N. Ireland 2
N. Ireland 1 Sweden 2
Norway 2 N. Ireland 1
N. Ireland 3 Norway 0
Sweden 3 Norway 1
Norway 0 Sweden 2

	P	W	D	L	F. A.	Pts
Yugoslavia	6	5	0	1	12. 4	10
N. Ireland	6	3	0	3	8. 5	6
Sweden	6	3	0	3	8. 9	6
Norway	6	1	0	5	5.15	2

Group 4.

Spain 1 Romania 1
Romania 2 Spain 2
Spain 1 Scotland 1
Scotland 1 Spain 2
Spain 2 Denmark 0
Denmark 1 Spain 2
Romania 1 Scotland 1
Scotland 1 Romania 1
Romania 6 Denmark 1
Denmark 0 Romania 0
Scotland 3 Denmark 1
Denmark 0 Scotland 1

	P	W	D	L	F. A.	Pts
Spain	6	3	3	0	10. 6	9
Romania	6	1	5	0	11. 6	7
Scotland	6	2	3	1	8. 6	7
Denmark	6	0	1	5	3.14	1

Group 5.

Holland 3 Poland 0
Poland 4 Holland 1
Holland 3 Italy 1
Italy 1 Holland 0
Holland 4 Finland 1
Finland 1 Holland 3
Poland 0 Italy 0
Italy 0 Poland 0
Poland 3 Finland 0
Finland 1 Poland 2
Italy 0 Finland 0
Finland 0 Italy 1

	P	W	D	L	F. A.	Pts
Holland	6	4	0	2	14. 8	8
Poland	6	3	2	1	9. 5	8
Italy	6	2	3	1	3. 3	7
Finland	6	0	1	5	3.13	1

Group 6.

Russia 2 Eire 1
Eire 3 Russia 0
Russia 3 Turkey 0
Turkey 1 Russia 0
Russia 4 Switzerland 1
Switzerland 0 Russia 1
Eire 4 Turkey 0
Turkey 1 Eire 1
Eire 2 Switzerland 1
Switzerland 1 Eire 0
Turkey 2 Switzerland 1
Switzerland 1 Turkey 1

Group 6 Final table:

	P	W	D	L	F. A.	Pts
Russia	6	4	0	2	10. 6	8
Eire	6	3	1	2	11. 5	7
Turkey	6	2	2	2	5.10	6
Switzerland	6	1	1	4	5.10	3

Group 7.

Belgium 1 East Germany 2
East Germany 0 Belgium 0
Belgium 2 France 1
France 0 Belgium 0
Belgium 1 Iceland 0
Iceland 0 Belgium 2
East Germany 2 France 1
France 2 East Germany 2
East Germany 1 Iceland 1
Iceland 2 East Germany 1
France 3 Iceland 0
Iceland 0 France 0

	P	W	D	L	F. A.	Pts
Belgium	6	3	2	1	6. 3	8
East Germany	6	2	3	1	8. 7	7
France	6	1	3	2	7. 6	5
Iceland	6	1	2	3	3. 8	4

Group 8.

West Germany 1 Greece 1
Greece 2 West Germany 2
West Germany 1 Bulgaria 0
Bulgaria 1 West Germany 1
West Germany 8 Malta 0
Malta 0 West Germany 1
Greece 2 Bulgaria 1
Bulgaria 3 Greece 3
Greece 4 Malta 0
Malta 2 Greece 0
Bulgaria 5 Malta 0
Malta 0 Bulgaria 2

	P	W	D	L	F. A.	Pts
West Germany	6	3	3	0	14. 4	9
Greece	6	2	3	1	12. 9	7
Bulgaria	6	2	2	2	12. 7	7
Malta	6	1	0	5	2.20	2

Dutch centre forward, Kist (white shirt) fights a lone battle against the Czech defence in the 1980 final stages.

Quarter-finals:

Czechoslovakia 2 Russia 0
Russia 2 Czechoslovakia 2

Holland 5 Belgium 0
Belgium 1 Holland 2

Spain 1 West Germany 1
West Germany 2 Spain 0

Yugoslavia 2 Wales 0
Wales 1 Yugoslavia 1

Final stages in Yugoslavia

Semi-finals

Belgrade.

Yugoslavia 2 — West German 4 (after extra time)
Popivoda, Dzajic — Flohe, Müller (D) (3)

Yugoslavia: Petrovic; Buljan, Muzinic; Oblak (Vladic), Katalinski, Zungul; Popivoda, Jerkovic, Surjak, Acimovic (Perusovic), Dzajic.

West Germany: Maier; Vogts, Dietz; Schwarzenbeck, Beckenbauer, Danner (Flohe); Wimmer (Müller (D)), Hoeness, Beer, Bonhof, Holzenbein.

Zagreb

Czechoslovakia 3 — Holland 1 (after extra time)
Ondrus, Nehoda, Vesely (F) — Ondrus (own goal)

Czechoslovakia: Viktor; Pivarnik, Gogh; Dobias, Ondrus, Capkovic (Jozef) (Jurkemik); Masny, Panenka, Nehoda, Moder (Vesely (F)), Pollak.

Holland: Schrijvers; Suurbier, Krol; Neeskens, Rijsbergen (Van Hanegem), Van Kraay; Rep (Geels), Van der Kerkhoff (W), Cruyff, Jansen, Rensenbrink.

Belgrade.

Final:

Czechoslovakia 2 — West Germany 2 (after extra time)
Svehlik, Dobias — Müller (D), Holzenbein

Czechoslovakia: Viktor; Pivarnik, Gogh; Dobias (Vesely (F)), Ondrus, Capkovic (Jozef); Masny, Panenka, Svehlik (Jurkemik), Moder, Nehoda.

West Germany: Maier; Vogts, Dietz; Schwarzenbeck, Beckenbauer, Beer (Bongartz); Wimmer (Flohe), Hoeness, Müller (D), Bonhof, Holzenbein.

Czechoslovakia won on penalties.

Zagreb.

Play-off for Third Place:

Yugoslavia 2 — Holland 3 (after extra time)
Katalinski, Dzajic — Geels (2), Van der Kerkhoff (W)

Yugoslavia: Petrovic; Buljan, Muzinic; Oblak, Katalinski, Zungul (Halilhodzic); Popivoda, Jerkovic, Surjak, Acimovic (Vladic), Dzajic.

Holland: Schrijvers: Suurbier, Krol; Arntz (Kist), Van Kraay, Jansen (Meutstege); Van der Kerkhoff (R), Van der Kerkhoff (W), Geels, Peters, Rensenbrink.

1980. Winners: (West Germany)

Qualifying round:

Group 1.

Denmark 3 Eire 3
Eire 2 Denmark 0
Eire 0 N. Ireland 0
N. Ireland 1 Eire 0
Denmark 3 England 4
England 1 Denmark 0
Denmark 2 Bulgaria 2
Bulgaria 3 Denmark 0
Eire 1 England 1
England 2 Eire 0
N. Ireland 2 Denmark 1
Denmark 4 N. Ireland 0
Bulgaria 0 N. Ireland 2
N. Ireland 2 Bulgaria 0
Bulgaria 1 Eire 0
Eire 3 Bulgaria 0
England 4 N. Ireland 0
N. Ireland 1 England 5
Bulgaria 0 England 3
England 2 Bulgaria 0

	P	W	D	L	F. A.	Pts
England	8	7	1	0	22. 5	15
N. Ireland	8	4	1	3	8.14	9
Eire	8	2	3	3	9. 8	7
Bulgaria	8	2	1	5	6.14	5
Denmark	8	1	2	5	13.17	4

Czech right winger Masny (dark shirt) bursts through the Dutch defence in Milan.

Group 2.

Norway 0 Austria 2
Austria 4 Norway 0
Belgium 1 Norway 1
Norway 1 Belgium 2
Austria 3 Scotland 2
Scotland 1 Austria 1
Portugal 1 Belgium 1
Belgium 2 Portugal 0
Scotland 3 Norway 2
Norway 0 Scotland 4
Austria 1 Portugal 2
Portugal 1 Austria 2
Portugal 1 Scotland 0
Scotland 4 Portugal 1
Belgium 1 Austria 1
Austria 0 Belgium 0
Norway 0 Portugal 1
Portugal 3 Norway 1
Belgium 2 Scotland 0
Scotland 1 Belgium 3

	P	W	D	L	F. A.	Pts
Belgium	8	4	4	0	12. 5	12
Austria	8	4	3	1	14. 7	11
Portugal	8	4	1	3	10.11	9
Scotland	8	3	1	4	15.13	7
Norway	8	0	1	7	5.20	1

Group 4.

Iceland 0 Poland 2
Poland 2 Iceland 0
Holland 3 Iceland 0
Iceland 0 Holland 4
East Germany 3 Iceland 1
Iceland 0 East Germany 3
Switzerland 1 Holland 3
Holland 3 Switzerland 0
Holland 3 East Germany 0
East Germany 2 Holland 3
Poland 2 Switzerland 0
Switzerland 0 Poland 2
East Germany 2 Poland 1
Poland 1 East Germany 1
Poland 2 Holland 0
Holland 1 Poland 1
Switzerland 0 East Germany 2
East Germany 5 Switzerland 2
Switzerland 2 Iceland 0
Iceland 1 Switzerland 2

	P	W	D	L	F. A.	Pts
Holland	8	6	1	1	20. 6	13
Poland	8	5	2	1	13. 4	12
East Germany	8	5	1	2	18.11	11
Switzerland	8	2	0	6	7.18	4
Iceland	8	0	0	8	2.21	0

Group 3.

Yugoslavia 1 Spain 2
Spain 0 Yugoslavia 1
Romania 3 Yugoslavia 2
Yugoslavia 2 Romania 1
Spain 1 Romania 0
Romania 2 Spain 2
Spain 5 Cyprus 0
Cyprus 1 Spain 3
Cyprus 0 Yugoslavia 3
Yugoslavia 5 Cyprus 0
Cyprus 1 Romania 1
Romania 2 Cyprus 0

	P	W	D	L	F. A.	Pts
Spain	6	4	1	1	13. 5	9
Yugoslavia	6	4	0	2	14. 6	8
Romania	6	2	2	2	9. 8	6
Cyprus	6	0	1	5	2.19	1

Group 5.

France 2 Sweden 2
Sweden 1 France 3
Sweden 1 Czechoslovakia 3
Czechoslovakia 4 Sweden 1
Luxembourg 1 France 3
France 3 Luxembourg 0
Czechoslovakia 2 France 0
France 2 Czechoslovakia 1
Luxembourg 0 Czechoslovakia 3
Czechoslovakia 4 Luxembourg 0
Sweden 3 Luxembourg 0
Luxembourg 1 Sweden 1

	P	W	D	L	F. A.	Pts
Czechoslovakia	6	5	0	1	17. 4	10
France	6	4	1	1	13. 7	9
Sweden	6	1	2	3	9.13	4
Luxembourg	6	0	1	5	2.17	1

Group 6.

Finland 3 Greece 0
Greece 8 Finland 1
Finland 2 Hungary 1
Hungary 3 Finland 1
Russia 2 Greece 0
Greece 1 Russia 0
Hungary 2 Russia 0
Russia 2 Hungary 2
Greece 4 Hungary 1
Hungary 0 Greece 0
Finland 1 Russia 1
Russia 2 Finland 2

	P	W	D	L	F.	A.	Pts
Greece	6	3	1	2	13.	7	7
Hungary	6	2	2	2	9.	9	6
Finland	6	2	2	2	10.	15	6
Russia	6	1	3	2	7.	8	5

Group 7.

Malta 0 West Germany 0
West Germany 8 Malta 0
Turkey 0 West Germany 0
West Germany 2 Turkey 0
Wales 0 West Germany 2
West Germany 5 Wales 1
Wales 7 Malta 0
Malta 0 Wales 2
Wales 1 Turkey 0
Turkey 1 Wales 0
Turkey 2 Malta 1
Malta 1 Turkey 2

	P	W	D	L	F.	A.	Pts
West Germany	6	4	2	0	17.	1	10
Turkey	6	3	1	2	5.	5	7
Wales	6	3	0	3	11.	8	6
Malta	6	0	1	5	2.	21	1

Italy qualified automatically as host nation.

Final stages in Italy.

Group 1.

Rome.

West Germany 1 Czechoslovakia 0
Rummenigge

West Germany: Schumacher; Kaltz, Dietz; Förster (B) (Magath), Cullmann, Förster (K.H.); Rummenigge, Stielike, Alloffs (K), Müller (H), Briegel.

Czechoslovakia: Netolicka; Barmos, Gogh; Stambacher, Ondrus, Jurkemik; Kozak, Panenka, Vizek, Gajdusek (Masny), Nehoda.

Naples.

Holland 1 Greece 0
Kist (Pen)

Holland: Schrijvers (Doesburg); Wijnstekers, Hovenkamp; Stevens, Van der Korput, Krol; Van der Kerkhoff (R), Van der Kerkhoff (W), Kist, Haan, Vreijsen (Nanninga).

Greece: Konstantinou; Kirastas, Iosifidis; Terzanidis, Kapsis, Firos; Mavros, Livathinos, Kouis, Ardizoglou (Anastopoulos), Kostikos (Galakos).

Hovenkamp of Holland (white shirt (3)) intercepts a loose ball in the 1–1 draw against Czechoslovakia in Milan.

Czech goalkeeper Netolicka punches clear against Holland watched by sweeper Ondrus (dark shirt, facing the camera).

1980 Final stages, Group 1 (continued)

Rome.

Czechoslovakia 3 — Greece 1
Panenka, Vizek, Nehoda — Anastopoulos

Czechoslovakia: Seman; Barmos, Gogh; Jurkemik, Ondrus, Berger (Licka); Masny, Kozak, Nehoda (Gajdusek), Panenka, Vizek.

Greece: Konstantinou; Kirastas, Iosifidis; Terzanidis (Galakos), Kapsis, Firos; Mavros, Livathinos, Kouis, Anastopoulos, Kostikos (Xanthopoulos).

Turin.

West Germany 0 — Greece 0

West Germany: Schumacher; Kaltz, Förster (B) (Votava); Cullmann, Stielike, Förster (K.H.); Rummenigge (Del' Haye), Memering, Hrubesch, Müller (H), Briegel.

Greece: Poupakis; Gounaris, Xanthopoulos; Nikoloudis (Koudas), Ravousis, Nikolaous; Mavros (Kostikos), Livathinos, Kouis, Ardizoglou, Galakos.

Naples.

West Germany 3 — Holland 2
Allofs (K) (3) — Rep (Pen), Van der Kerkhoff (W)

West Germany: Schumacher; Kaltz, Dietz (Mattaüs); Schuster, Förster (K.H.), Stielike:; Rummenigge, Briegel, Hrubesch, Müller (H) (Magath), Allofs (K).

Holland: Schrijvers; Wijnstekers, Hovenkamp (Nanninga); Stevens, Van der Korput, Krol; Van der Kerkhoff (R), Van der Kerkhoff (W), Kist (Thijssen), Haan, Rep.

Milan.

Czechoslovakia 1 — Holland 1
Nehoda — Kist

Czechoslovakia: Netolicka; Barmos, Gogh; Jurkemik, Ondrus, Vojacek; Masny (Licka), Kozak, Nehoda, Panenka (Stambacher), Vizek.

Holland: Schrijvers; Wijnstekers, Hovenkamp; Thijssen, Van der Korput, Krol; Rep, Van der Kerkhoff (W), Nanninga (Haan), Poortvliet, Van der Kerkhoff (R) (Kist).

Greece (dark shirts) counter-attack against Czechoslovakia in the 1980 final stages

Group 1 (continued)

Final table:

	P	W	D	L	F.	A.	Pts
West Germany	3	2	1	0	4.	2	5
Czechoslovakia	3	1	1	1	4.	3	3
Holland	3	1	1	1	4.	4	3
Greece	3	0	1	2	1.	4	1

Group 2.

Turin.

Italy 1 England 0
Tardelli

Italy: Zoff; Gentile, Benetti; Oriali, Collovati, Scirea; Causio (Baresi (G)), Tardelli, Graziani, Antognoni, Bettega.

England: Shilton; Neal, Sansom; Thompson, Watson, Wilkins; Coppell, Keegan, Birtles (Mariner), Woodcock, Kennedy.

Naples.

England 2 Spain 1
Brooking, Woodcock Dani (Pen)

England: Clemence; Anderson (Cherry), Mills; Thompson, Watson, Wilkins; McDermott, Hoddle (Mariner), Keegan, Woodcock, Brooking.

Spain: Arconada; Uria, Gordillo; Zamora (Dani), Olmo, Alesanco; Juanito, Saura, Santillana, Cundi, Cardenosa (Carrasco).

Rome.

Italy 0 Belgium 0

Italy: Zoff; Gentile, Benetti; Oriali (Altobelli), Collovati, Scirea; Causio, Tardelli, Graziani, Antognoni (Baresi (G)), Bettega.

Belgium: Pfaff; Gerets, Renquin; Cools, Meeuws, Millecamps; Van der Elst, Van Moer (Verheyen), Mommens (Van den Bergh), Van der Eycken, Ceulemans.

Turin.

England 1 Belgium 1
Wilkins Ceulemans

England: Clemence; Neal, Sansom; Thompson, Watson, Wilkins; Coppell (McDermott), Keegan, Johnson (Kennedy), Woodcock, Brooking.

Belgium: Pfaff; Gerets, Renquin; Cools, Meeuws, Millecamps; Van der Elst, Van Moer (Mommens), Van den Bergh, Van der Eycken, Ceulemans.

Milan.

Italy 0 Spain 0

Italy: Zoff; Gentile, Cabrini (Benetti); Oriali, Collovati, Scirea; Causio, Tardelli, Graziani, Antognoni, Bettega.

Spain: Arconada; Tendillo, Gordillo; Zamora, Migueli, Alesanco; Dani (Juanito), Saura, Satrustegui, Asensi, Quini.

Milan.

Belgium 2 Spain 1
Gerets, Cools Quini

Belgium: Pfaff; Gerets, Renquin; Cools, Meeuws, Millecamps; Van der Elst, Van Moer (Mommens), Van den Bergh (Verheyen), Van der Eycken, Ceulemans.

Spain: Arconada; Tendillo (Carrasco), Gordillo; Zamora, Migueli, Alesanco; Juanito, Saura, Satrustegui, Asensi (Del Bosque), Quini.

Final table:

	P	W	D	L	F.	A.	Pts
Belgium	3	1	2	0	3.	2	4
Italy	3	1	2	0	1.	0	4
England	3	1	1	1	3.	3	3
Spain	3	0	1	2	2.	4	1

England's Trevor Brooking clashes with Wilfred Van Moer, the Belgian veteran, who was thought by some international critics to be the best player in the 1980 final stages.

Rome.

Final.

West Germany 2 — Belgium 1
Hrubesch (2) — Van der Eycken (Pen)

West Germany: Schumacher; Kaltz, Dietz; Schuster, Förster (K.H.), Stielike; Rummenigge, Briegel (Cullmann), Hrubesch, Müller (H), Allofs (K).

Belgium: Pfaff; Gerets, Renquin; Cools, Meeuws, Millecamps; Van der Elst, Van Moer, Mommens, Van der Eycken, Ceulemans.

Naples.

Play-off for Third Place.

Italy 1 — Czechoslovakia 1
Graziani — Jurkemik

Italy: Zoff; Gentile, Cabrini; Altobelli, Collovati, Scirea; Causio, Tardelli, Graziani, Baresi (G), Bettega (Benetti).

Czechoslovakia: Netolicka; Barmos, Gogh; Jurkemik, Ondrus, Vojacek; Masny, Kozak, Nehoda, Panenka, Vizek (Gajdusek).

Czechoslovakia won on penalties.

Uli Stielike (centre, white shirt) of 1980 European champions, West Germany, throws a feint to bewilder Czech defenders.